SILENT CHRONICLES: MY NAME IS VICTORY

I0151152

Dr. Carla A. Murphy

Empower

Publishing

Empower Publishing
302 Ricks Drive
Winston-Salem, NC 27103

First Empower Publishing Books edition published November, 2025
Empower Publishing, Feather Pen, and all production design are trademarks.

For information regarding bulk purchases of this book, digital purchase and special discounts, please contact the publisher at publish.empower.now@gmail.com

Cover design by David Blackburn

Manufactured in the United States of America
ISBN 978-1-63066-629-3

Acknowledgement

We appreciate the prayers, trust, and loving dedicated teamwork of our amazing Co-Authors, also known as Team Genesis.

The powerful testimonies of these phenomenal Co-Authors helped to strengthen and encourage one another to press past their pain.

We are extremely grateful for the prayers of our Moderators, Pastors, and Great Lakes Baptist Association Leaders.

Special thanks to our families for supporting the vision while we sacrificed time to write our stories, for truly, our voices count.

We are certainly grateful for:

- Empower Publishing, which provided outstanding publishing service.

- Supporter Rev. Frank Bostic and Pilgrim Missionary Baptist Church for opening their doors to host our Book Launch.

- Cover Creator Mr. David Blackburn, for your contribution to turning our vision into reality.

- Encouragers Ms. Letizia Conrad and Ms. Linda Prince Roberts, who encouraged us to write the vision and make it plain, to tell our stories.

- Supporter Ms. Bertha Ann Robinson for her prayers and presence.

- Writing Coaches for their inspirational support, editing, and sharing helpful writing tips to enhance the authors' stories.

- Supervisor Brenda W. Billups of Rochester, New York

- Supervisor Shelia Pinckney of Buffalo, New York

- Dr. Johnique Billups Atkins of Houston, Texas

- Mr. Jamal Donaldson Briggs of Charlotte, North Carolina

Finally, we wish to thank every reader for honoring us by reading our book. We hope that something was written that will help you to know that you can also have Victory through Our Father Jesus Christ, Our Lord.

So, we sincerely extend our heartfelt thanks to everyone who contributed to making this project a great success. Although we have written this anthology "Silent Chronicles: My Name Is Victory", we all had a major part to play in this project, so you can be sure that Your Name Is Victory, Too.

Warm Regards

Introduction:

Have you ever felt like your mind was playing tricks on you? Do you feel stuck, hurt, disillusioned, or confused? Have you forgotten that trouble doesn't always last? If so, you are not alone. "Silent Chronicles: My Name Is Victory" was written by ten amazing, courageous, and transparent young adults in the Western New York Great Lakes Region.

Their stories are thought-provoking, heart-warming, and powerful testimonies of what God can do when you trust Him. Each chapter identifies a scripture and a theme that will encourage the reader to reflect and record their reaction, thoughts, prayers, and additional encouragement for future consideration.

They have learned that silence can be deafening and destructive when it is mismanaged. Silence can be detrimental to one's health if not handled properly. The authors speak with boldness and clarity about their assurance and faithfulness of the Loving God that we serve. They take a holistic approach to fighting their negative feelings, self-doubt, and disappointments.

The Co-Authors have experienced moments of trials, tribulations, and heartache. This collection of stories is a source of healing for anyone who feels alone or in the wilderness. Their stories will help the reader to be mindful that freedom is available to all through Jesus Christ our Lord. Their challenges helped the authors to feel a shift, a new beginning, as they persevered with resilience to become unstoppable.

Our challenge is that you take a leap of faith. Embrace your life story. Dive into a journey of self-discovery, healing, deliverance, and personal freedom that will be treasured for a lifetime. Tell your testimony. Your voice counts. Your story is priceless; it is uniquely valuable. Take a moment to think about all the wonderful things that God has done for you in your life. Remember to celebrate every step forward, every opportunity, and every blessing. Practice walking by faith and not by sight. Declare, "I will bless the LORD at all times: His praise shall continually be in my mouth." (King James Version—KJV)

Your Name Is Victory!

Table of Contents

Tribute: Rev. Dr. Dennis Lee Jr.

This book is dedicated to the Great Lakes Baptist Association, Inc., Moderator, Reverend Dr. Dennis Lee, Jr.

He is the husband of Lady Paulette Lee, a loving father, grandfather, and the proud Pastor of Hopewell Baptist Church in Buffalo, New York.

Moderator Lee is a kind, caring, and committed Spiritual Leader. He has faithfully served in the United States Armed Forces. Now, he serves as a dynamic leader in the Service of the Lord.

Moderator Lee is a bold and courageous visionary leader. He encourages everyone around him to press on in unity. He is open-minded, intuitive, innovative, and responsive to the needs of people.

Moderator Lee is a great example of how to lead with excellence, discernment, and consistency. He is a major supporter, especially of the children, youth, and young adults of the Great Lakes.

We have watched Moderator Lee as he has successfully led his family, church, and the Baptist Ministers' Conference of Buffalo and Vicinity.

He has also served the Empire Baptist Missionary Convention of New York, Inc., and the National Baptist Convention, USA, Incorporated with excellence.

Moderator Dennis Lee Jr. is a tremendous transformational trendsetter. So, the Youth and Young Adults of the Great Lakes would like to sincerely thank Moderator Lee for being a great Christian Example. We have witnessed your Faith in Action as you have trusted us with a great responsibility to serve independently in the Association with love, joy, and peace.

We appreciate you, and we honor you. Your loving support will be treasured for the rest of our lives. So, we hope that although thank you may seem so small, you will feel the sentiments of our hearts.

Congratulations, Moderator Dennis Lee Jr., for a job well done, and we thank you for your service. We love you and Lady Paulette Lee.

With Love and Prayers,

The Great Lakes Baptist Association, Inc. Youth and Young Adults

Preface By David Blackburn

Silent Chronicles: My Name Is Victory

The journey of life brings with it both challenge and triumph. The desire to see tomorrow is defined by a simple, but powerful force called hope.

These ten authors are fortunate enough to stand on a foundation built by the Author of faith, hope, and love. They have chosen to share their stories, not just as survivors of life's trials, but as victors— testimonies in motion.

Matthew 11:28 declares:

"Come unto me, all ye that labour and are heavy laden, and I will give you rest."

As a child, I enjoyed the sound of this verse, as a man, I enjoyed the promise of this verse.

The voices represented in these pages paint vivid portraits of success & struggle. Their testimonies reveal the power of pressing forward while standing on the promises of God. As readers of these journeys, we don't just observe from a distance, but we partake in the victory of each author.

Imagine this: that parts of their stories were born so that we might live more victoriously.

- **Struggle → Deliverance**
- **Doubt → Faith**
- **Pain → Purpose**
- **Obstacles → Milestones**
- **Fear → Freedom**
- **Waiting → Prosperity**
- **Calling → Trusting God's Way**

As you bear witness to these silent chronicles, celebrate the victories as family in this life journey, and share belief in the goodness & greatness of our Lord!

Tatiyana Monique Williams, a dynamic individual proudly born and raised in Rochester, New York. She is the cherished daughter of Keisha Coleman and Lonzo Williams. A distinguished alumna of School Without Walls, where she graduated in 2015, Tatiyana furthered her academic journey at both Genesee Community College and Monroe Community College. Professionally, she is a Certified Nursing Assistant (CNA) and is a Certified Phlebotomist, demonstrating her commitment to healthcare.

 Beyond her medical pursuits, Tatiyana is a driven entrepreneur, the proud owner of Elite Beauty and Elite, LLC. Through her businesses, she passionately crafts custom T-shirts, offers expert monogramming services, and creates a delightful variety of treats, taking immense pride in the quality and creativity of her work.

Her commitment extends deeply into her community, a member of Mt. Vernon Missionary Baptist Church, Tatiyana actively contributes to the Nurses Guild. Her exceptional leadership skills were evident as the Past President of the Youth Ministry for the Great Lakes Baptist Association, a role she ascended to after serving as its dedicated secretary. She has also lent her valuable support to the Security Ministry within the Empire State Convention.

When not dedicating her time to her professional and community endeavors, Tatiyana indulges her passion for travel and meeting new people. Cruising holds a special place in her heart as her favorite mode of exploration, having taken her to enchanting destinations like Paris,

Hawaii, Mexico, and the Bahamas, alongside numerous vibrant cities across the United States. She also possesses a beautiful singing voice, which she loves to share.

Tatiyana's influence and accomplishments are further highlighted by her distinction as one of the inaugural Queens in the prestigious Brothers' and Sisters in Christ Program for the Great Lakes Baptist Association. She is also an esteemed member of the Sylvester Anderson Voices to be Heard Toastmasters Club, where she continually hones her communication and leadership skills, truly embodying the spirit of "Members Matter."

Tatiyana is the evidence of the word "Unstoppable".

Discovering Your True Identity by Tatiyana Monique Williams.

"Learning Who You Are Through Life's Experiences"

From my earliest recollections, the intricate dance of decision making has been a constant companion. As a child, I quickly grasped that decisions are synonymous with choices, and true choices demand thoughtful deliberation to ensure the path taken is the right one. Occasionally, this required a deeper dive, a bit of research, to illuminate the optimal direction. My nascent years were marked by a perplexing dilemma: where would I truly live and attend school? I often found myself questioning why the adults around me didn't offer clearer guidance.

My mother's frequent visits to Rochester often culminated in my return to Atlanta. These transitions were met with a mix of emotions – sometimes tears, sometimes a quiet acceptance. Yet, a week or two later, an undeniable longing for Rochester would lead me to my aunt, prompting a call to my mother and an arranged flight back. This pattern became a summer ritual until one pivotal year. My mother, breaking the cycle, enrolled me in fourth grade in Atlanta, despite my aunt's premonition that this would ensure I stayed. This decision, made for me, left a profound sense of unease. How could I articulate my discomfort to my mother? The Rochester School, understandably weary of my late starts each academic year, added to the tension. That particular school year in Atlanta was fraught with misery, and by its close, I was just shy of the points needed to advance. A significant discussion with the school administration eventually secured my promotion, and I swiftly departed Atlanta, never to revisit that particular academic predicament. Once I was able to exercise my own agency, I proactively arranged my return to Rochester.

I also learned that life is not all about me, but I am the important one in my life. Therefore, I have to be the best I can. I don't say if I am successful, I say when I am successful. Others around me can & will benefit from my sharing and giving back my life experiences. I don't plan to live my life as a role model, but as one that can be recognized for the difference I make in the business & fashion world.

My Mentor taught me early in life to dance to the beat of my own drum. With that thought, I learn my choices are my own, and if I don't succeed, it will be on me. For me, that is not an option. Another thought I carry with me from another mentor is, "I can help you, show you, but I won't do it for you." When you take the positive things in life, choices are better made.

My journey continued, marked by a high school graduation and the pursuit of higher education. My initial aspiration for law gradually shifted towards medicine, though neither fully captured my longterm vision. I earned my license as a Certified Nursing Assistant, gaining invaluable experience and the opportunity to travel. Subsequently, I certified as a Phlebotomist, before settling into my current role as a Dental Office Assistant.

Beyond my professional roles, I am a testament to self-made entrepreneurship, guided by divine inspiration. My hands find purpose in creation: I sew, cook, and bake with passion. I design and print custom T-shirts, craft delectable sweet treats, and offer eyelash artistry services – continually expanding my creative ventures.

Through every twist and turn, I've cultivated essential life wisdom. The foremost lesson is to truly know oneself, to understand your inherent strengths and passions. Embrace what you do with joy and conviction. Choose to align your efforts with the divine plan laid out for you. Yes, dare to explore new avenues, venture to different places, and broaden your horizons. Cultivate inner peace and confidence, walking proudly in your authenticity. Strive to leave an indelible mark on the world, one that genuinely reflects who you are. And to achieve this, the cornerstone remains: "Know who you are." For me, that identity is unequivocally "Unstoppable." As the scriptures affirm, "With Christ, I can do all things."

Theme: Unstoppable

1 Corinthians 15:57-58 KJV

But thanks be to God, which giveth us the victory through our Lord Jesus Christ.

Therefore, my beloved brethren, be ye steadfast, unmovable, always abounding in the work of the Lord, forasmuch as ye know that your labour is not in vain in the Lord.

_____

_____

_____

_____

_____

_____

_____

_____

_____

_____

_____

_____

_____

_____

_____

_____

_____

_____

Christian Hurdle was born and raised in Rochester, New York, and is the second oldest of five siblings. Growing up in a close-knit family taught him the value of responsibility, empathy, and lifting others up. As a quiet and observant child, Christian found his voice through singing, performing, and creative expression, which helped him grow into the confident and purpose-driven leader he is today.

Christian currently works in higher education, where he supports students and contributes to creating fair, accessible, and encouraging learning environments. He also serves as President of the Young People's Auxiliary and contributes to his church's media team, using creativity and faith to inspire and support others.

Driven by faith and a desire to make a positive impact, Christian is passionate about helping

Others discover their gifts, overcome challenges, and use their talents to serve with excellence.

Crushing Doubt with the Power of Scripture by Christian Hurdle

"Faith does not make things easy, it makes them possible."

Luke 1:37

My journey began in quiet observation. From my earliest memories, silence was my companion, a natural inclination that led me to keep to myself. My mother often recounts how, as a young child, my conversations were exclusively reserved for her and my beloved godmothers. It was no great revelation, then, that I would grow into a soft-spoken, naturally shy individual, content to remain in the background, far from the spotlight.

Yet, a subtle shift occurred within me during my high school years. Stepping onto the stage to sing in church and perform in theatrical productions ignited an unexpected spark. The spotlight, initially daunting, became a conduit for confidence, a liberating space where I could express emotions and ideas I had never dared to voice aloud. It was there, under those lights, that I began to discover my voice— not merely in a literal sense, but in understanding who I was destined to be.

Life, however, has a profound way of testing such newfound growth. When I ventured from home to pursue college in Michigan, I encountered the stark realities and unexpected challenges of independence. This transition brought with it a wave of anxiety unlike anything I had experienced before. Being from the familiar, and with my identity in an unfamiliar landscape, and witnessing peers seemingly navigate their paths with effortless grace while I felt perpetually stuck, began to take a significant toll. This past year, that undercurrent of anxiety surged to an unbearable peak. I found myself wrestling with troubling thoughts, questioning my very purpose, looking in the mirror and disliking the reflection, and constantly comparing my journey to everyone else's. I felt adrift, profoundly lost, and utterly exhausted by the pretense that I was managing just fine.

That breaking point, however, became an unexpected turning point. I realized I could no longer continue on the same trajectory; a different path was essential. This realization propelled me back into a deeper, more intentional relationship with God. I stopped merely "going through the motions" and instead plunged wholeheartedly into His Word, seeking solace and direction.

Several passages became anchors for my soul. Isaiah 41:10, "Do not fear, for I am with you; do not be dismayed, for I am your God," resonated deeply, a powerful reminder that even in my deepest solitude, I was never truly alone. Philippians 4:6-7 offered a practical balm for my anxious mind: "Do not be anxious about anything, but in every situation, by prayer and petition, with thanksgiving, present your requests to God." And 2 Timothy 1:7, declaring, "For God has not given us a spirit of fear, but of power, love, and a sound mind," became a personal declaration, a truth I spoke over myself whenever fear attempted to reclaim its hold.

But perhaps the most transformative influence wasn't a verse at all, but a simple prayer—The Serenity Prayer. Interestingly, it's my mother's cherished prayer, and through my own struggles, it has now become deeply significant to me too: "God, grant me the serenity to accept the things I cannot change, Courage to change the things I can, And wisdom to know the difference." This prayer became my daily mantra, a profound reminder that perfection is not a prerequisite for progress, and that it is not only permissible but essential to extend grace to myself as I navigate the messy, beautiful process of growth.

Looking back, I can honestly say that conquering anxiety was not an overnight victory. It remains an ongoing journey, a muscle I continue to strengthen. Yet, through this experience, I have unearthed invaluable strategies for crushing doubt whenever it arises. I've learned the profound importance of radical honesty— with myself, and with God. I've discovered the immense power of speaking scripture over my circumstances, knowing that God's Word far outweighs any fear, lie, or insecurity I might tell myself. I've embraced the critical role of leaning into my community—my family, friends, and mentors—who lovingly speak life into me when my own spirit falters. And most importantly, I've come to understand that growth often manifests in subtle ways. Sometimes, it's simply the act of showing up again after a difficult day, choosing to remember that I am chosen, deeply loved, and fully equipped, even when my feelings suggest otherwise.

Today, I am compelled to share my story, using my experiences to encourage other young individuals who may be navigating similar battles. Whether through ministry engagements or simply in candid conversations, my hope is to convey that it's perfectly alright not to have all the answers, and to affirm that doubt, while persistent, does not have the final say.

If there is one singular message I wish for others to take away from my narrative, it is this: doubt can be overcome through the unwavering power of faith. You only need to allow the resonant truth of God's Word to be louder than your deepest worries. If I were to distill my life's evolving narrative into a single word, it would unequivocally be "Assurance." For no matter how uncertain or turbulent life may become, I have learned to find profound rest in the assurance that God is continually with me, guiding my steps, fortifying my spirit, and constantly reminding me that His divine plan is always infinitely greater than any fear I may face.

Theme: Assurance

1 Thessalonians 1:5 KJV

For our gospel came not unto you in word only, but also in power, and in the Holy Ghost, and in much assurance; as ye know what manner of men we were among you for your sake.

_____

_____

_____

_____

_____

_____

_____

_____

_____

_____

_____

_____

_____

_____

_____

_____

_____

_____

Atu Tramel is an erudite scholar currently engaged in multidisciplinary studies at Roberts Wesleyan University, an institution renowned for its commitment to academic rigor and spiritual development. His academic pursuits span the captivating intersections of Business, Psychology, and Homeland Security, allowing him to develop a versatile and dynamic skillset.

Tramel's academic voyage began at Northstar Christian Academy, where he successfully completed his secondary education, laying a robust foundation for his current pursuits. His intellectual curiosity extends beyond the confines of conventional education, evident in his growing interest in the fashion and design industry. This passion has led him to develop skills in graphic design, a discipline that harmoniously marries aesthetics and functionality.

Born into the spiritual embrace of Mt. Vernon Baptist Church, Tramel's faith has been a guiding beacon in his journey. Christened and deeply embedded in this nurturing religious community, he continually contributes to the Church's initiatives with unwavering commitment. His faith and dedication are a testament to his character, reflecting his deep-seated values of service, community, and spiritual growth.

In the entrepreneurial realm, Tramel's ventures are as diverse as his academic endeavors, encompassing modeling, graphic design, and landscaping. These pursuits not only represent his broad interests but also underscore his drive to turn passion into tangible action. He is one who fervently believes in continual learning, and this belief permeates all aspects of his life.

Tramel's love for learning extends beyond the academic sphere into the realm of personal growth and well-being. His pursuit of knowledge in health and wellness reveals a holistic approach to life, an approach that prioritizes not just intellectual growth but also physical and spiritual well-being.

In essence, Atu Tramel is not merely a student, an entrepreneur, or a faithful church member; he is a lifelong learner pursuing a holistic path of growth and development. His journey is a testament to the power of passion, commitment, and a ceaseless desire to learn and grow.

Patience to Prosperity by Atu Tramel

"Keep Moving Forward." Martin Luther King

In a world that thrives on speed, where instant gratification often overshadows enduring growth, patience has become one of the rarest virtues to cultivate. Yet in the divine order of life, patience is not merely a moral quality; it is the bridge between promise and prosperity. The path to success, fulfillment, and spiritual abundance is rarely swift or simple. True prosperity—both material and spiritual—demands a steady faith, a calm endurance, and the willingness to trust God's timing over our own. The Bible, particularly in the King James Version, repeatedly reminds us that prosperity is not only the fruit of labor but the reward of steadfast patience.

The Foundation of Patience

Patience, at its essence, is trust in motion. It is the evidence of faith expressed through endurance. The Apostle Paul writes,
"But if we hope for that we see not, then do we with patience wait for it" (Romans 8:25, KJV). This verse captures the spiritual foundation of patience—it is the act of waiting with hope. Hope without patience is wishful thinking; patience

22

without hope is passive resignation. Together, they form a powerful force that aligns our desires with divine timing.

In the modern sense, patience is often misunderstood as inactivity or delay. Yet biblically, patience is not idleness—it is perseverance under pressure. James writes, "Knowing this, that the trying of your faith worketh patience. But let patience have her perfect work, that ye may be perfect and entire, wanting nothing" (James 1:3–4, KJV). Patience refines the believer. It shapes character, strengthens faith, and prepares the heart to handle the blessings that are to come.

Prosperity without patience is premature and can lead to destruction. But when patience has completed its work, prosperity follows in due season.

The Process of Waiting

God often allows waiting seasons to test and temper the human heart. Every promise He gives carries a process attached to it. The story of Abraham illustrates this truth perfectly. God promised Abraham that he would be the father of many nations, yet twenty-five years passed before Isaac, the child of promise, was born. During that time, Abraham had to learn to wait without wavering. As Romans 4:20–21 declares, "He staggered not at the promise of God through unbelief; but was strong in faith, giving glory to God; And being fully persuaded that what he had promised, he was able also to perform."

Patience transforms waiting from frustration into formation. In waiting, God forms character, wisdom, and resilience. Abraham's patience produced more than a child—it produced faith that would inspire generations. Similarly, David was anointed king as a shepherd boy but waited years before sitting on the throne. Joseph dreamed of leadership but was sold into slavery and imprisoned before ruling Egypt. Their stories teach us that God's promises are true, but His timing is perfect. Prosperity that lasts is built through processes that test endurance.

Patience as a Spiritual Investment

Just as a seed must spend time in the soil before bearing fruit, so must faith be cultivated through patience before it prospers. The Psalmist

23

beautifully describes this principle: "They that sow in tears shall reap in joy" (Psalm 126:5, KJV). The tears represent toil, waiting, and unseen labor; the joy represents the harvest that patience brings. God is not unjust—He rewards those who diligently seek Him and those who wait upon Him.

Hebrews 6:12 echoes this truth: "That ye be not slothful, but followers of them who through faith and patience inherit the promises." Prosperity is inherited, not instantly attained. Faith opens the door, but patience walks through it. Every believer must understand that divine prosperity is not only about material gain but spiritual growth—peace, wisdom, and fulfillment. Without patience, prosperity loses its purity and purpose.

The Blessing Hidden in Delay

One of the hardest lessons to embrace is that delay is not denial. God's timing often appears delayed to human eyes, yet His delays are divine preparations. Isaiah 40:31 encourages us, "But they that wait upon the Lord shall renew their strength; they shall mount up with wings as eagles; they shall run, and not be weary; and they shall walk, and not faint." Waiting renews strength because it transfers control from man to God. When we rush, we rely on our own abilities; when we wait, we rely on His sovereignty.

In every delay, God develops something greater within us. He may be preparing the environment, shaping our character, or removing obstacles unseen to us. When we are patient, we position ourselves to receive His best rather than our own limited version of success. What seems like a setback is often a setup for something far greater. The delay is where maturity grows and destiny aligns.

The Character of Prosperity

Many equate prosperity with wealth, status, or material possessions. Yet biblical prosperity is holistic—it includes peace, purpose, health, and favor. "Beloved, I wish above all things that thou mayest prosper and be in health, even as thy soul prospereth" (3 John 1:2, KJV). God's desire for prosperity is rooted in the prosperity of the soul. Without inner wholeness, outer wealth becomes meaningless. Patience cultivates that inner prosperity by teaching contentment, gratitude, and humility.

When one learns to wait on God, they develop trust in His process rather than anxiety about outcomes. Prosperity without patience can lead to pride; prosperity born through patience produces gratitude. Every blessing gained through endurance carries the fragrance of faith. The believer who prospers through patience knows that every step, every struggle, and every silent season had a divine purpose.

From Endurance to Harvest

In the book of Galatians, the Apostle Paul reminds believers of the law of sowing and reaping:
"And let us not be weary in well doing: for in due season we shall reap, if we faint not"
(Galatians 6:9, KJV). This verse captures the essence of the journey from patience to prosperity.

The phrase "due season" implies a divine timetable. We may sow good works, faith, or effort, but the harvest belongs to God's appointed season. The condition, however, is that we "faint not." Endurance is the key to unlocking divine timing.

Prosperity is not given to the impatient but to those who persist despite delay. The harvest of patience is sweet because it is hard-earned and divinely appointed. When prosperity arrives through God's timing, it sustains itself. It does not crumble under pressure because it has been built through trials that purified and prepared the heart.

Practical Application: Living Out Patience

To live out patience is to walk daily in surrender. It is to trust God even when results are unseen, and to remain faithful in the small things. Prayer, gratitude, and perseverance are the daily disciplines that keep patience alive. When we replace comparison with contentment and haste with humility, we align ourselves with divine prosperity.

We can take encouragement from the farmer who plants a seed, knowing that growth is invisible before it becomes visible. He does not dig it up daily to check progress—he waters it, protects it, and trusts time to do its work. Likewise, we must trust that God is working beneath the surface of our circumstances. "Be patient, therefore, brethren, unto the coming of the Lord. Behold, the husbandman waiteth for the precious fruit of the earth, and hath long patience for it" (James 5:7, KJV). This imagery reminds us that every delay carries hidden growth.

Conclusion: The Reward of Patience

Patience is not passive-it is powerful. It is the silent strength that transforms faith into fulfillment. Those who wait on God never wait in vain, for His timing is perfect, His promises are sure, and His prosperity is complete. The journey from patience to prosperity refines the heart, deepens faith, and glorifies God through the testimony of endurance.

In the end, prosperity is not merely what we gain but who we become in the process of waiting.

As Proverbs 10:22 declares, "The blessing of the Lord, it maketh rich, and he addeth no sorrow with it." When we let patience do her perfect work, we inherit prosperity that brings peace, joy, and divine satisfaction—prosperity not only of possession, but of spirit.

Theme: Perseverance

James 1:4-5 KJV

But let patience have her perfect work, that ye may be perfect and entire, wanting nothing. If any of you lack wisdom, let him ask of God, that giveth to all men liberally, and upbraideth not; and it shall be given him.

_____

_____

_____

_____

_____

_____

_____

_____

My name is Daijah Lashae Blackburn, and I was born in the late 1990s in Toledo, Ohio. My parents are Denika Blackburn (Hutchen) and David Blackburn. I am number two of six beautiful individuals— four of whom are my sisters and one of whom is my brother (I call them my "Built-in Besties"). Most of my earliest memories are in Buffalo, New York, where my Dad's family is from. I lived there full-time during the years of my parents' marriage. The year I turned four, I moved to Toledo with my mom and siblings, and from that point on, my life was like a crossover episode of two shows that couldn't be more different from one another. The only common denominator was the love of Jesus.

I thank God for wonderful parents who exposed me to love and Jesus at a young age. They always spoke life into me and taught me right from wrong. I always get compliments on how my parents did a great job with me. As the young folks would put it, they really snapped. I appreciate that I had so many siblings who taught me so much about life. I have five people who went through similar obstacles, trials, and traumas whom I can be myself around, and I love that. I also thank God for my Sweetie, my Gran, Papa, Granny, and Great Gran, who all had a tremendous impact on my upbringing. I wouldn't be who I am without them, my aunts, uncles, beautiful cousins, and friends.

I remember the day I publicly proclaimed my belief in Jesus. I was sitting with my mom in the front section of the middle row at Eastern Star Baptist Church. I remember whispering in my mom's ear that I wanted to sing with the choir. She said something like "okay, but you have to join the church." I had no problem with that. During that time when the doors of the church were opened, my mom took me up. While I may not have understood the significance of it all at the time, I knew what I needed to know. My pastor at the time, Dr. John W. Williams, asked me two questions. If I recall correctly, they were: (1) Do you believe in Jesus? (2) Do you believe that he died for your sins and rose on the third day? Two easy yeses. I was baptized at four years old. Looking back, I am so thankful for the foundation I got in church. By Kindergarten, my memory held scriptures like Psalm 23, Matthew 6:33, John 9:4, and Romans 8:28. While I may not have understood their depth, they built me so strong that I rely on them even now.

I would be remiss if I did not also mention the profound impact that Greater Hope Baptist Church (Dr. James C. Blackburn, Jr.), The Armory Church (Bishop William James), and Macedonia Baptist Church (Pastor Herman Alston, Jr.) had on my upbringing. I was filled with the Word throughout my childhood and teenage years.

To this day, it flows from me as a stream of living water. (*See* John 7:38)

As far as school was concerned, I always did pretty well. People always told me I was very smart, so I never had a reason to believe I couldn't do the work in front of me. That doesn't mean I never slacked off or got beside myself, but the words of life spoken over me made me academically successful at every level of life. I was always on the Principal's/Dean's list and Honor Roll, and in High School, I was a member of the National Honor Society.

I remember during one National Honor Society meeting, our advisor, Mrs. Bridgett Smith, announced that she was holding an election for President. I watched all my peers as they got ready to campaign (I had no interest in running for anything). Not many days after that, Mrs. Smith peeped into my second-period AP Government class, saying that she needed me to sign something. She had me sign a document as the President of our chapter of the National Honor Society and stated that I was the only student who did enough for the organization to be in the position. It's amazing how God works. Even when I didn't run, He still put me over it.

That opportunity opened the door for me to lead service in my high school and to develop the beautiful gift that God gave me to speak. Not only did I speak at the subsequent induction, but I gave the best graduation welcome anyone ever heard.

As far as extracurriculars went, I was an orchestra student who played the violin from the first grade until the second semester of sixth grade, when I switched to the cello. To this day, the cello is my favorite instrument (besides my voice, of course). I played the cello very consistently until college, when I began playing the trombone. I also ran cross country, track, was a cheerleader, and served as the captain of the soccer team. I was never really a star at those things, but I loved to be active and athletic.

Another great opportunity I got in high school was to be presented as a cotillion debutante, and sure enough, by God's grace, I was crowned Miss Debutante 2016. At my high school senior awards ceremony, I earned Outstanding Senior Female, School Service Award, Highest Science Score in my class for the Ohio Graduation Test, Musicianship for Orchestra, and Top Seven Graduate.

Upon graduation from High School, I began studying at Spelman College in Atlanta, Georgia. I studied English (after switching from Economics), and I loved it. I love to read and write, and I thank God that my studies at Spelman challenged me to deepen and refine those skills. I thank God for women like Dr. Donna Akiba Harper and Dr. Michelle Hite, who did not know they were like mothers to me in their capacities as teachers. They taught me how to think critically about the world around me, and they taught me about agape love.

As far as grades went, I earned a 2.5 GPA my very first semester, and got my last B+ during the first semester of my sophomore year. From that point on, I only earned A's and A-'s. In my final semester, I earned

31

a 4.0 and finished with an overall 3.5 (cum laude). It was not as high an honor as I would have liked to achieve, but it was certainly an accomplishment upheld by the grace of God.

I took a gap year before attending law school, and I thank God for Dr. Deanna Kortesky, my 18th-century British Literature Professor, who helped me draft my personal statement prior to graduation. In 2021, I enrolled in Penn State Law in University Park, Pennsylvania.

During my first year of law school, I was on the winning team for the 2022 Mid-Atlantic Constance Baker Motley Mock Trial Competition. Through that experience, I became an active member of Penn State Law's chapter of the Black Law Students Association ("BLSA"). I loved the BLSA community and its mission to foster love, growth, and upliftment for Black law students. In 2022, I was elected chapter Vice-President, and in 2023, I was elected Director of the Constance Baker Motley Mock Trial Competition for the Mid-Atlantic Region of the National Black Law Students Association.

While in law school, I also served as co-chair of the Criminal Law Society's 2023 Criminal Justice Reform Conference. I also taught students at State College High School as a part of the "Street Law" course, for which I also earned a Cali award. That was my absolute favorite law school "in-class" experience. I loved interacting with students and centering them in the teaching process. Not only did it give me the opportunity to teach them, but I got to learn from them, too. That's a skill I eventually adopted as a Vacation Bible School and Sunday School teacher.

During law school, I also got the opportunity to work for multiple judges and complete multiple legal internships. I thank God for every opportunity and every leader who made an impact on me. I'd like to especially recognize Franklin R. Pratcher, Esq., the Honorable Shakura Ingram, Kristin LaVoy, Esq., Efrain Marimon, J.D., the Honorable Linda T. Walker, and the Honorable Karen Roby.

I thank God for my law school journey because it taught me how to think and work smarter than I ever thought I could. I graduated in 2024 and passed the July 2024 Uniform Bar Exam. In January 2025, I was sworn into the New York Bar and began practicing law in Buffalo, New York.

Despite all my secular accomplishments, my favorite thing about life is church. I am a grateful member of the Greater Hope Baptist Church in Buffalo, New York. I thank God for the opportunity to serve as a Sunday School teacher, nurse, praise team and choir member, and kitchen staff member. I am also grateful for the role Project Impact continues to play in my walk with Christ.

I love the fellowship and worship that come with being a part of the body of Christ. There is no work more important to me than that which pertains to the building of the Kingdom of God. Amen.

Breaking Free: Walking in Deliverance and Freedom by Daijah Lashae Blackburn

Come unto me, all ye who labor and are heavy laden, and I will give you rest.

- Jesus Christ (Matthew 11:28)

There's this girl I used to know, but I don't know her anymore. She was beautiful, and I really wanted to admire her. She was determined and headstrong, but she felt like she had something to prove. As a matter of fact, she did way too much trying to prove herself to others— as if she could prove her worth to herself by proving it to other people. Before she knew it, she turned from a sweet and confident girl to a bittersweet and insecure lady. She was super independent and truly believed that her way was the best way. Her way was not the best way, and she learned that lesson the Jonah way. The devil is a liar and a pretty good one, but he was never a match for our God, Jehovah. Not even close.

The girl, my "Old Homegirl" if you will, was raised in love. She grew up in the textbook definition of a broken home, but she could never say she didn't have a family that loved her. They raised her in the

33

nurture and admonition of the Lord (*see* Ephesians 6:3) and played no games when it came to discipline. It only took a few hand pops and butt whoopings for my Old Homegirl to learn obedience fast. She could hardly stand the chastisement and the fussing, so she did exactly what she was told or, at the very least, made it look like she did. I don't think the chastisement made my Old Homegirl feel unloved, but I believe it gave her the perception that she had to earn love with good behavior. That's a dangerous mindset for anyone to have.

If I could go back in time, I'd tell my Old Homegirl that perfect love is not to be earned, and that it is exercised despite our shortcomings.

I would tell her that God's love toward us never fails, even when we do, and His mercies and compassion toward us are new every morning (*See* Lamentations 3:22-23). I'd even go as far as the writer of Hebrews and declare to her that no chastening seems good in the present, but it yields peaceable fruit to those trained by it. (Hebrews 12:11). Maybe then she would have known that "being good" was never a source of true love.

My Old Homegirl never really fit in either. I remember as far back as pre-school, she could play alone with no problem. It's not like she never made friends, but as soon as the groups started forming, she was the oddball out. God gave her friends throughout the years, and even in the seemingly true friend groups she had, she often found herself the object of bullying. Perhaps it was because she was small and non-confrontational (and perhaps because she bullied her own sister), but God was teaching her something all along. As she matured, family was the only group she felt a true sense of belonging to (they were oddballs too), and at some point, she didn't belong with them— at least not physically.

When she left home to attend college, my Old Homegirl found that moving to a popular city to attend a school full of beautiful and intelligent Black women didn't change the fact that she didn't belong with the crowds. After four long weeks, she found herself emotional and wanting. A day came when she got an opportunity to join an organization where she got to do something she loved in a group of people who were perhaps as socially weird as she was. On the other hand, that organization was overcome with what the Bible calls "evil communications." As Paul writes in I Corinthians 15:33, "Be not deceived: evil communications corrupt good manners." Contrary to Paul's advice, my Old Homegirl was deceived, and her manners were totally corrupted.

If I could go back in time, I'd tell my Old Homegirl to wait on the Lord, and that the reason she never fit in was not because she wasn't good enough. She didn't fit in because she was of "a chosen generation, a royal priesthood, [a] holy nation, [and] a peculiar people." (I Peter 2:9).

I would tell her she was called to demonstrate the glory of God at every step, and she was too good to forget the royalty she truly was. I'd also tell her perfect love was her portion and that the Lord set her apart to do great things. I'd tell her that the cure to her feelings of loneliness was in Him all along, and I would have asked the Lord to keep her from being tempted by those feelings. They say hindsight is 20/20.

In all actuality, my Old Homegirl was living life her own way, and it was an emotional rollercoaster with super high highs and super low lows. She was having the time of her life while simultaneously living in spiritual misery (if you know, you know).

My Old Homegirl was mentally and physically bound like a real prisoner in a real jail. As hard as life was hitting her, though, she mastered the art of making it seem like she had it all together. She masked spiritual bondage with high grades, charisma, and good looks. You know I hate to give him too much credit, but the devil is really good at making lies look pretty.

In 2020, my Old Homegirl hit her first rock bottom. It was crazy and ugly. She spent days and nights overcome with tears from attacks from the outside and from the inside. She felt worthless, like she couldn't do anything right. After all the changes she made to herself trying to belong, she still felt alone. That's when she decided it was time to start reading her Bible for real, like Genesis to Revelation for real. I think

35

she came to the conclusion that she didn't have a choice. It was either that or die.

Reading the Bible the long way taught my Old Homegirl wisdom. It seemed much easier for her to conduct herself like a fool when she didn't realize that foolish ways were foolish. Go figure. I saw the fruit of it in her life, and after three long years of a very obvious fight with depression and anxiety, my Old Homegirl found peace.

In 2021, she went on to do great things on a whole new level. My Old Homegirl applied and entered into a special doctorate program where she was in line to become one of 2% of Black women in the United States in her profession. Even though the Lord got her there, she somehow felt intimidated. So intimidated that she started to have some sort of an identity crisis.

It's not that she didn't believe she belonged, but she didn't believe she was good enough as she was. Insecurity took over her mind, and she became more anxious, flustered, and disorganized than ever.

If I could go back in time, I'd tell my Old Homegirl that it was a mistake for her to believe that she was better off cutting back on Bible time to make room for the school work that eventually overwhelmed her life. I would remind her of the beautiful promises written in Joshua 1:8-9 and Psalm 1:1-3 (Please pause and read them). Had she relied on those promises, I just know she would've conquered that program with peace at the top of her class— but she lived and she learned.

By the first semester of her last year in the program, my Old Homegirl hit a whole new low. Perhaps not as dramatic and tearyeyed as the previous rock bottom, but a very sophisticated hell on earth. She was spending a lot of time with characters that I would describe as spiritual vampires. Her cup was running empty while she bore the weight of the world on her shoulders. She was desperate to the point that she finally gave up. She didn't give up on life, but she gave up the belief that she needed to control it.

Ahh, surrender. Selah

In November 2023, my Old Homegirl made a verbal commitment to present her body as a living sacrifice to the LORD. (*See* Romans 12:1-2). In January 2024, she changed her lifestyle to match that verbal commitment. She was carrying so much dead weight that God never intended for her to carry. From actual trauma, to consequences of her poor choices, to things that were never in her control— she learned how to turn problems over to the LORD. Little by little, God increased her faith, and with that, she started to give up the behaviors, patterns, and people that brought destruction to her inner woman. She took on a whole new life, which she never imagined and which she never thought she wanted. On the other side of surrender and obedience, my Old Homegirl discovered a freedom she never knew existed.

I always saw myself in my Old Homegirl, and that's why I never gave up on her. She was never really the people's choice, but she was always God's. One thing about our God is that He will keep you when you belong to Him, and He will leave the ninety-nine just to get *you*. (*See* Matthew 18:12).

I am not my Old Homegirl anymore, but she was always becoming me. I was shackled and chained when Christ showed me who I was and who I was destined to be. *Royalty.* Now I understand the Samaritan woman's testimony, and dare I say unto you, "Come see a man who told me everything I ever did." (John 4:29). He *is* the Christ, and He can save you from *anything*. (*See* John 4:30.) It was one thing to believe Christ died for me, but it was another thing to let Him set me free. That's the difference between believing in Him and *being* in Him. Freedom.

In freedom, I know I lack nothing because my Father owns EVERYTHING, and He loved me so much that he gave me Jesus to pay for it all. I know love, peace, joy, gentleness, hope, goodness, faith, temperance, and long suffering are my portion. (*See* Galatians 5:22-23). I live in the True Vine and walk in the shadow of the Almighty, knowing that no circumstance, no matter how painful or inconvenient, can take away the fullness of joy that comes from being in the presence of the LORD. (*See* John 15; Psalm 91:1; Psalm 27:5; Psalm 16:7). I'd rather cry sad tears in the presence of Jesus than to happily laugh in the company of the enemy. I'm so glad I took my freedom in Christ, and I dare you to take yours too. (*See* Matthew 7:7).

There's this girl I used to know, but perhaps I never knew her at all. . . *"if any [wo]man be in Christ,[s]he is a new creature: old things are passed away; behold, all things are become new."*

Theme: Freedom

John 8:32 KJV

And ye shall know the truth, and the truth shall make you free.

Shainna Overstreet is a dynamic and results-driven professional with expertise in restorative practices, workforce development, alternative education, and holistic student support. She is deeply committed to creating impactful learning environments, fostering community engagement, and implementing innovative wellness strategies that empower students to achieve both academic and personal success.

Born and raised in Buffalo, New York, Shainna is the proud daughter of Melissa (Bruce) Gainey and Omar Kareem Overstreet Sr., and the beloved goddaughter of Audrey and Jacob Harris Jr. From an early age, she has been grounded in faith, family, and service. A lifelong member of Greater Hope Baptist Church, she grew up under the spiritual guidance of her great uncle, Pastor James C. Blackburn Jr. In 2005, she participated in a life-changing mission trip to Juarez, Mexico, where she served in community outreach— an experience that strengthened her compassion and deepened her desire to help others.

Professionally, Shainna serves as the Director of Wellness and Academic Coordinator at Peace of the City Ministries in Buffalo, NY, where she oversees wellness initiatives, develops individualized learning programs, and collaborates with educators and families to ensure wraparound support for at-risk youth. Prior to this role, she led Alternative Education at Health Sciences Charter School, where she designed and implemented a structured program supporting students facing behavioral, attendance, and safety challenges. Her earlier work as a Lead Credible Messenger and Parent Partner with the Community Credible Messenger Initiative showcased her ability to lead restorative circles, implement trauma-informed care, and guide youth toward positive transformation.

Beyond her professional endeavors, Shainna has served faithfully as a Youth Minister at Greater Hope Baptist Church since 2018, organizing plays, Bible studies, and community outreach events to uplift and mentor the next generation.

Currently pursuing a Bachelor of Arts in Psychology at Canisius College (expected January 2027), Shainna maintains a 3.5 GPA and has achieved Dean's List honors for four consecutive semesters. She is also a proud member of the Psi Chi International Honor Society in Psychology.

Throughout her career, Shainna has been recognized for her leadership, community service, and dedication to youth development. Her honors include the Good Samaritan Award for outstanding service assisting parents and students during the COVID-19 pandemic and the Leadership Award for excellence in education and mentorship. She also celebrates a remarkable 90% success rate in her alternative education and youth mentorship initiatives.

Above all, Shainna finds her greatest joy in her role as a devoted mother to her three beautiful children—Thomas Frazier IV and twins Se'arlait and ShiAnne Frazier. Her journey reflects faith, resilience, and an unwavering commitment to empowering others through education, compassion, and restorative connection.

Overcoming: Turning Mountains into Milestones by Shainna Overstreet

"Do not be conformed to this world, but be transformed by the renewal of your mind, that by testing you may discern what is the will of God—what is good and acceptable and perfect."—

Romans 12:2 (ESV)

Sometimes I find myself on my knees, hands pressed to my head, crying out for God to touch and heal my mind. I know He can give me anything I ask for—He is able—but if my mind isn't renewed, I cannot receive it. I can't hold it, cherish it, or walk fully in it. God could bless me with everything I've prayed for, yet if my thoughts remain unhealed, I'll miss the joy of it entirely.

From the earliest days of my childhood, I felt a deep connection with God. A woman once told me that my self-talk as a little girl was really just a conversation with Him—and she was right. I've always spoken to God plainly, honestly, like a friend who listens without judgment. But there were seasons when my mouth felt glued shut, when my prayers stayed locked behind my teeth. Those were the days when disappointment and shame sat heavy on my chest. I thought silence might protect me from judgment, but even when I couldn't find words, my tears became prayers. I'd whisper, "Lord, please catch them."

Every heartbreak, every season of wandering, every dark night of the soul was preparation for the life He was shaping for me.

The Early Church Years

My mountain didn't begin in college—it began long before that, in high school. But my roots, my strength, came from the church.

Growing up at **Greater Hope Baptist Church**, under the leadership of Rev. Dr. James C. Blackburn Jr.—my great-uncle—it wasn't just a place of worship. It was home. Family. Foundation. My grandmother, *Gram*, made sure I was there every time the doors opened. She lived close enough that if we had to, we walked.

Church taught me discipline, service, and belonging. Sunday school, choir rehearsals, Bible study, revivals—those were my routines. I ushered, sang, served in pastoral care, and even learned to wash dishes in the church kitchen. I didn't just grow up in the church—I grew because of it.

The sanctuary itself held stories in its walls. Blush pink carpet under our feet, matching choir robes, the hum of the organ warming the air before service began. I loved sitting near the front, close enough to feel the inspiration of the music. Singing brought me joy—it was the closest I felt to God. When Pastor would sing *"My Soul Has Been Anchored,"* everything in me settled. I knew, somehow, that everything was going to be alright.

Lessons from the Kingdom Girls

At eight years old, I begged for permission to join the choir. Pastor hesitated at first, but eventually, I was allowed to wear the robe. That robe wasn't just fabric—it was a commitment. To serve God. To live the words I sang. To strive daily to be more like Him.

Every Sunday, the first thing you saw when you stepped into the sanctuary was the tithing box. I learned early that giving back wasn't just about money—it was about offering your first fruits: your time, your talents, your increase. *Malachi 3:10* became real to me: *"Bring ye all the tithes into the storehouse…"* It was a lesson in trust, humility, and obedience.

We young ladies were known as **Kingdom Girls**, a name given by my aunt and Sunday school teacher, *Aunt Audrey Harris*. She told us we were to live for Jesus—not in words only, but in heart, in action, in integrity. She'd often quote *Matthew 5:37*: *"Let your communication be yea, yea; nay, nay."* Her teaching wasn't gentle—it was alive, full of fire. She'd point her manicured finger and say, *"Shainna, you've got to live right!"* Her voice still echoes in my spirit. And she was right. Living right wasn't about perfection—it was about alignment. It was about positioning myself where God's blessings could find me.

The Spark and the Search

Even as I grew in the church, I hungered for something more—attention, validation, belonging. I wanted people to see me the way I felt seen by God inside those four walls. I wish someone had told me that the joy I felt there couldn't be found anywhere else, but even if they had, I'm not sure I would've listened.

That search led me to high school—a battlefield of intellect, anger, and identity.

I wanted to be noticed, but I reached for it in the wrong ways: fighting, rebelling, chasing risks that made me feel powerful for a moment but left lasting scars. I was kicked out freshman year for fighting. Junior year—again. Yet somehow, by the grace of God, I graduated in 2006 at the top of my class, with over $40,000 in scholarships. But the anger and pain I carried didn't disappear with that diploma. It followed me, like an invisible weight pressing on my shoulders.

High School Hustle

I wasn't a "good student" in the traditional sense—I was just good at the system. My memory was sharp; if I saw something once, I could recall it forever. My mom had taught me early, maybe in third grade, to break words apart, find the root, and understand the meaning. That small lesson turned into a strategy. I didn't study—I just remembered.

But socially, I never felt like enough. Not pretty enough. Not stylish enough. Just smart—and even that stopped impressing people after a while. I learned to perform. I was loud, funny, the class clown by eighth grade. It was my armor, a way to hide the insecurity that lived under my skin.

By high school, my "Kingdom Girl" confidence clashed with my craving for acceptance. I didn't turn the other cheek-I swung back.

I went to four high schools, two of them alternative programs, fighting my way through each one. And yet-I never missed the honor roll. Even in rebellion, God's hand was steady over my academics.

44

Still, I was lost. Alone. My Sunday school teachers couldn't reach me anymore. My friends liked me because I fought for them, not because they knew me. I embarrassed my mom, kept her awake at night, and deep down, I embarrassed myself.

But even through that storm, the seed of purpose planted in me at Greater Hope Baptist never died-it was just buried for a time.

The Climb & Redemption

When I got to Canisius College, I thought I was ready. I had worked hard, earned my accolades, and walked through doors that some thought I'd never reach. But readiness isn't just about opportunityit's about mindset. My mind, shaped by survival and scarcity, was still learning peace. There's a strange comfort in dysfunction when it's all you've ever known. The excitement of new beginnings collided with the quiet anxiety of old patterns that refused to let go.

I wasn't disciplined-I was talented. And talent will only take you so far when the mind is weary. I didn't study because I'd never had to. My memory carried me, my charm covered me, but neither could sustain me. I was good at playing the system, but I had never learned how to master myself. Then came the dismissal.

The Fall

The day I walked across that basement tunnel to the dean's office, my stomach churned, my hands trembled, my heart thudded in my chest. Every step echoed with the sound of failure and fear. *How did I let this happen?* I thought of every moment I'd disappointed my mother, every time I'd made her defend me, every promise I'd made to do better.

When Mrs. Dudley spoke - "You are no longer a student at Canisius College" - her words moved in slow motion. My ears rang, my vision blurred, my spirit deflated. The walls closed in as shame whispered, You failed again.

Walking out, I traced my fingers along the blue and gold walls, looking for something solid. But there was nothing to hold on to - just the tunnel, the cold air, and the echo of my own questions. I wanted to call my best friend Nic, the one who knew my heart and my prayers, but shame kept me silent. Isolation felt safer than confession.

The weight of expectation - family, church, community - pressed down heavy. I felt like I had lost not just my place in school, but my place in the story God was writing for me.

But even in that silence, God whispered. Not loudly, not through thunder or wind - just a still, steady truth in my spirit: Your mountain isn't Canisius. Your mountain is your mind.

Naming the Mountain

It took years to understand that my failures weren't the end - they were the mirror. My habits, my need for approval, my fear of not being enough - they all pointed back to a mountain I had been circling for years. Naming it was the first step to climbing it.

God wasn't punishing me; He was positioning me. Every loss was an instruction. Every disappointment was discipline. The wilderness that followed my dismissal wasn't wasted - it became the training ground for the woman I am today.

I wandered, searching for belonging in people and places that couldn't sustain me. I tried to fill my emptiness with acceptance, validation, and control - but nothing fit. The further I drifted, the louder God's pull became.

Through each heartbreak, each closed door, I began to recognize the same quiet pattern: God was teaching me how to surrender. How to trust. How to renew my mind.

Lessons from the Wilderness

In that wilderness, I began to see the steps that would change my life:

1. **Name the mountain.** I had to face my truth - my pain, my pride, my unhealed mind. Denial only delayed the climb.

2. **Lean on God.** When words failed, prayer became my breath. I learned that even silence can be sacred when you trust that God hears the whispers of your heart.

3. **Take small steps.** Discipline became my daily offering - organization, consistency, faithfulness. I celebrated the small wins because those built the strength for bigger ones.

4. **Learn from the wilderness.** Every failure became a teacher. Every season of waiting taught me resilience.

5. **Use your story to lift others.** When I began to share my journey - the falls, the grace, the recovery - it became a bridge for others still in their valleys. My testimony gave my pain purpose.

Return and Redemption

Years later, with trembling faith, I reapplied to Canisius College - the same place I once left in shame. I prayed, waited, and trusted that if it was God's will, the door would open again.

And it did.

I was accepted. My scholarship was restored. The same campus that once witnessed my defeat has now become the stage for my redemption. I walked those familiar tunnels again - but this time, with peace. I carried not shame, but gratitude. I knew who I was and whose I was.

But the moment was bittersweet. I learned that Mrs. Dudley, my mentor and champion, had passed away. How I wished I could sit across from her again and say, *"I did it. You were right about me."* Her belief in me still echoes in my heart - a reminder that God places people in our lives to water the seeds He's already planted.

The Whole Story

Looking back, I see how every season—childhood, rebellion, dismissal, redemption—was stitched together by God's faithfulness. My story was never just about overcoming failure; it was about becoming whole.

Even now, when I wish I were further along - owning a home, reaching certain milestones - I pause and give thanks. God has been good. His timing has been perfect. I sit in expectation, not because I've earned it, but because He is a promise keeper.

He took the broken, the wandering, the angry, and the unsure - and made her whole. He turned my mourning into dancing, my mountains into milestones. And now, as I climb, I reach back to lift others, reminding them that their mountains can move too.

Living Proof

One word defines my journey: **Holistic.** Every trial, every triumph, every fall and rise are threads in the same tapestry. Nothing was wasted. God used it all - mind, body, and spirit - to make me whole.

Today, I stand as living proof of His mercy. My life is a testament to perseverance, to grace, to transformation.

Your struggles don't define you - your response to them does. The mountain is steep, the climb is long, but the view from the summit? It's breathtaking. Every tear, every stumble, every prayer was preparing you to shine. And as for me -

"I'm living proof of what the mercies of God can do. If you knew me then, you'd believe me now. He turned my whole life upside down, took the old me and made me new - that's what the mercies of God can do."
- "Mercy," Housefires Written by Nate Moore, Tony Brown, and Brandon Lake. © 2021 Heritage Worship Music Publishing / Tony Brown Music Designee / Bethel Music Publishing. Used with permission.

Theme: Holistic

Mark 12:30 KJV

And thou shalt love the Lord thy God with all thy heart, and with all thy soul, and with all thy mind, and with all thy strength: this is the first commandment.

Shoshana J. Williams is a native of New York City who was educated at Johnson City High School. She earned a Bachelor of Arts degree in Psychology from Daemen College. She also received a certificate of completion from the New York Legal Education program at Elisabeth Haub School of Law at Pace University. She later pursued further education and obtained her Master of Science in Leadership and Innovation with a focus on social impact organizations from Daemen University. She currently works for an agency that provides services to individuals with developmental disabilities.

Shoshana Williams is a humble servant of her Lord and Savior, Jesus Christ. She dedicates her time, talents, and gifts to the Hopewell Baptist Church, where she is a proud member. Shoshana serves as the assistant superintendent, teaches a primary Sunday School class, and leads reassembly. She enjoys working with children and involves them in events that spiritually lead. She is also an advisor for Vacation Bible School, where she creates various arts and crafts for youths ages five years old to young adults. She is also an advisor for the Youth Ministries. She leads the youth by attending various conferences, creating projects, events, parties, and various theatrical plays. She is also a member of the Young Adult Choir. She is a member of the Anniversary Committee and Hospitality Committee, where she assists in serving the congregation and fellow neighboring churches. Shoshana is the treasurer of the Nurses' Guild.

Shoshana is a member of the Angel Tree Ministries, where she assists with providing encouragement to children whose parents are incarcerated. She is also in charge of the Decorating Committee. She plans, decorates, and facilitates various church celebrations. Shoshana has inspired and built leadership skills in younger girls, having been a previous Girl Scout leader. She has volunteered with the Police Athletic League, Seneca Babcock Community Center, St. Vincent De Paul Soup Kitchen, Habitat for Humanity, Buffalo News Kids Day, Friends of the Night People, and the Buffalo Psychiatric Center. I participated in multiple walks in the city of Buffalo, NY, including but not limited to the Heart Walk, Turkey Trot, Charles McDougal Run, and various other fundraisers and charity events.

Shoshana Williams is also a powerful, enthusiastic, passionate PEF (Public Employee Federation) member. She is a prior union steward and second counsel leader for PEF Region 1, Division 167. Her previous constituency was located at the Getzville and Lockport Day Hab. Her hobbies are spending time helping others, reading, traveling, journaling, and swimming. Shoshana Williams is a daughter, sister, aunt, and godmother. She is a wonderful friend who gives all she can to help her family, friends, and others that she loves. She puts God first in all things and always gives thanks. She makes every day look easy because she trusts God in all things. Her resilience and strength empower others. She is the living example that "with God all things are possible." Her favorite scripture is

Philippians 4:6 (NLT): "Do not worry about anything. Instead, pray about everything, tell God what you need, and thank him for all he has done." She lives by Galatians 6:9 (NLT)"Let us not become weary in doing good, for at the proper time we will reap a harvest if we do not give up. She is now a co-author of the book entitled "Silent Chronicles: My Name is Victory" with the chapter called My Spiritual Journey: Lessons, Growth and Transformation.

My Spiritual Journey: Lessons, Growth and Transformation by Shoshana J. Williams

My spiritual journey began at a very young age. As a child, I followed Catholicism. As a little girl, my grandmother used to take me and my brother to a Catholic church in Manhattan. This Catholic church was a Cathedral. It was beautiful inside. This was not the only beautiful cathedral I saw growing up. I went to various Catholic schools that had huge Cathedrals affiliated with the school. Some of my memories growing up in the Catholic school system were my uniform.

I wore shiny black shoes, long navy-blue socks that came up to my knees, the white blouse, and the prep pleated plaid girls' skirt. In the winter, I wore a heavy navy-blue wool coat. At school, we used to break and go into the Catholic church where they spoke Latin. I was not familiar with the Latin language that was spoken at Mass. I did as I was told by the church, and that was to confess my sins in the confessional box, and that's what I did. At that young age, I don't believe I had too much to confess. Confused and out of place, I did not want to give up on learning just because I experienced difficulties, so I asked questions and received answers. This was the only way I was going to grow and transform into a better me. To transform, I need to feel comfortable with things that are unfamiliar.

As years went by, I was not satisfied with my spirituality, so I decided to do something about it. I became resilient and went out and chose to enhance my life by learning about various religions. Learning what religion was best suited for me. I did not want to give up on my hopes of being spiritually fed. After I obtained my bachelor's degree at Daemen College, my hopes were to find a place of worship in the city where I resided. I wanted to find a church that I could identify with, a church that felt like home. Possibly even a church, I knew everyone by face and name. I didn't want to feel lost and out of place. I wanted to feel the holy spirit and hear God's word. My ideal church would have substance, purpose, and be filled with imperfect people who were like me. If someone were to ask me a common question: Shoshana, what church do you belong to? I wanted to be able to answer boldly. After searching for a church, being invited by friends and coworkers, I began to feel hopeless. I went to churches in various parts of Buffalo that weren't too far from my home. Some friends recommended me to this church, and I visited that church, but I continued my search because I felt like I didn't belong to any of the churches I visited.

Everyone talks about their calling. I wanted to know what mine was. I do realize there is no perfect church, but I wanted a church that was perfect for me. I wanted to make an impact on others' lives. I wanted to show others what love was because I grew up in a household that showed me unconditional love. I not only love all my family members, but I like them all. I wanted to take on a task at the time that seemed big for me but not too big for God. I just didn't know how I was going to achieve this obstacle. Some of the things that I have done to keep a level head were to keep a positive social support system around me.

I did this by leaning on God for the discernment he gifted to me and from good friends and family members. I will use my life as an example for others through my good work. More time had passed, and I went to a church called the Hopewell Baptist Church. I visited for months before I became a member and was later baptized. I was a new creature. I was welcomed with open arms and cried like a baby during the right hand of fellowship. I knew I made the right decision for myself. I began joining various ministries in the church.

I became dedicated and passionate about being a servant for the Lord.

The Hopewell Baptist Church was there for me at my weakest moments. They were there for me when I was very sickly from COVID-19, my father passed away, and my diagnosis with cancer. I will always be forever grateful to the Pastor and the members of the church. I could not ask for a more supportive church family during that difficult time. My family and church family were very thoughtful, and there was nothing that I needed that I did not have. I felt so blessed. During this time, I persevered and was resilient through my struggles because I never lost focus on who God is. I was not scared because I know the strength and power God possesses. I was beyond grateful for all the kind gestures and acts of kindness everyone had shown me. Every time I had an issue, a sickness, or a challenge, my family and church were there for me.

One word that would describe my message is resilience. I am resilient because of my power to overcome challenges that I face during difficulties and adversities. I grew as a person when I began to say yes to the things I wanted to do. I looked for no other approval of how to do what Shoshana wanted to do. I accepted nothing less than what I deserved. I thank God for all the gifts, experiences, and people that he has placed in my life. I will forever be humble and grateful for each memory and each day I can wake up and be a part of others' lives by doing God's work here on earth.

A five-step process that I used to overcome the obstacles that others may benefit from is: trust in God, have faith in God, believe in yourself, show compassion for others, and lastly sow good seeds.

I truly believe man is not strong enough to block or interfere with what God has for someone. As the saying goes, "Man cannot close any doors God has opened for you, and a door will not close that God has opened for you". A message that I would like to uplift the reader with is my two scriptures from the bible. Which are Be resilient in everything you do, and with God all things are possible." Do not worry about anything. Instead, pray about everything, Tell God what you need, and thank him for all he has done." Philippians 4:6 (NLT). Start living by Galatians 6:9 (NLT) "Let us not become weary in doing good, for at the proper time we will reap a harvest if we do not give up.

If someone wants to contact me, I can be reached at Shoshanahall@yahoo.com.

Theme: Resilience

Philippians 4:13 KJV

I can do all things through Christ, which strengtheneth me.

_____

_____

_____

_____

_____

_____

_____

_____

_____

_____

_____

_____

_____

_____

_____

_____

_____

_____

_____

Raymond Anderson Jr. Raymond is not merely an individual of faith but a dynamic force of nature, embodying the spirit of a true "Fighter," a testament to the belief that "Won't God Do It" — a conviction often championed by Pastor Dion J. Watkins.

His life's journey is powerfully anchored in the scripture, Acts 16:25-28, reflecting his steadfast reliance on divine intervention.

Born on July 28th, 1985, to the late Nichole Jaycox Borden Anderson and Raymond Anderson Sr., Raymond's foundational years were steeped in a commitment to personal growth and service. A proud graduate of Bennett High School in 2003, he further honed his diverse talents by pursuing advanced education at the International Air & Hospitality Academy and earning a certificate in Culinary Arts from the Adult Division of the Buffalo Public School System. These early endeavors laid the groundwork for a career characterized by versatility and excellence.

Raymond's professional life is as multifaceted as his community engagement. He currently lends his expertise to the esteemed Avaniti Mansion, while also serving as a dedicated employee of the Mt. Olive Missionary Baptist Church of Lackawanna, New York, under the visionary leadership of Pastor Keith D. Mobley.

Demonstrating true entrepreneurial spirit, Raymond is also the proprietor of his own successful venture, God's Design, a desktop printing company.

Within the spiritual community, Raymond is a recognized pillar of strength and inspiration. His passion for worship shines through his roles as a praise & worship leader and choir director. Beyond the pulpit, he contributes significantly to the administrative staff, serves as a devoted deacon, and compassionately guides new members.

His influence extends beyond his local church; Raymond is also the Area Vice President of the Empire Missionary Baptist Convention Young People's Division, a vital member of the security team, and a respected figure within the Great Lakes Missionary Baptist Association, where he serves as a praise & worship leader, trustee, and oversees marketing and media initiatives. His commitment further extends to actively supporting and nurturing other ministries across the state of New York and far beyond its borders.

Despite his demanding schedule, Raymond remains deeply rooted in his family. As the eldest of five children—Raymond Jr., Bryanna, TaLiea, Karly, & Ezekiel—he cherishes his connections with his paternal grandparents, as well as a vast network of aunts, uncles, nieces, nephews, and cousins, embodying a strong family-oriented ethos.

Raymond's compassionate spirit is perhaps best exemplified by his unwavering dedication to community service. He is a committed volunteer for the National Kidney Foundation, the American Heart Association, and WNY HIV & AIDS initiatives. He also extends his empathy and wisdom by providing counseling to individuals in need, consistently demonstrating a willingness to help anyone he can, at any given time.

Raymond Anderson Jr.'s journey is one of profound resilience and indomitable faith. Even when faced with challenging medical conditions and the doubts of others, he lives by a powerful personal mantra encapsulated in Philippians 3:14: "I press toward the mark of the prize of the high calling of God in Christ Jesus." This scripture perfectly articulates his remarkable ability to overcome adversity with grace, strength, and unwavering spiritual conviction. Raymond is truly a beacon of hope, dedication, and selfless service.

Young, Anointed and Unstoppable: Doing Ministry God's Way by Raymond Anderson Jr.

"Fighter"

My journey, a tapestry woven with both blessings and formidable trials, has truly unveiled the boundless grace that makes one "Anointed and Unstoppable." It's a testament to discovering God's way, even when the path is shrouded in doubt.

I often reflect on my formative years, brimming with a youthful zeal for faith. Becoming a deacon in my church as a young adult, I carried a naive conviction that my devotion rendered me immune to hardship, believing God's grace was a protective shield against all tribulation. This prideful assumption, a hallmark of my younger self, felt utterly unshakable. Yet, as I traversed life with this misguided sense of invincibility, a quiet, profound realization began to surface. It was an inner voice, gently but firmly challenging my proud stance, whispering of the true nature of human vulnerability. It reminded me that while surrounded by loving family—mothers, fathers, grandparents, aunts, uncles, cousins, and friends—their power, like my own, was inherently limited. "Look to the hills, from whence comes your help," the wisdom echoed, pointing me toward an inexhaustible source.

This awakening coincided with a tangible shift in my world. Academic pursuits grew more demanding, and a wave of sickness began to touch loved ones. Initially, I rationalized these occurrences as the natural

60

progression of life and aging. But as my commitments expanded—at school, church, and within the community—my life became a recurring cycle of hospital visits, first for others, then increasingly for myself. The faces of nurses and doctors became intimately familiar. Lying in a hospital bed, a question echoed within me: "What do I do now?" It was in that vulnerable moment that I truly lifted my eyes and heart in prayer. "Lord, have mercy on me. Are you trying to tell me something?" Desperate for guidance, I reached for my phone, not for distraction, but to seek scripture. My search led me directly to the Lord's Prayer.

That night, a paradigm shift occurred. I didn't just recite words; I learned to pray with my whole being. Life was infused with new meaning, my spiritual walk deepened, and my perspective transformed. I understood, with unwavering clarity, that I was created to serve. This revelation ignited a fierce spirit within me, enabling me to defy medical prognoses and overcome significant health challenges. I became a fighter, not just for my physical wellbeing, but for the purpose I had found.

My passions reflect this spirit of service and exploration. I cherish the opportunity to travel beyond Buffalo, experiencing new places and cultures. These trips, whether yearly family excursions, solo adventures, or church conventions, have consistently broadened my horizons, even when they've occasionally necessitated hospital visits before my return home.

Through it all, prayer has been my constant companion, a source of strength and a guide for safe passage. One of my most profound sources of stress relief is singing. When I sing, I can cast off all burdens, lifting my voice to call upon the Master. My songs are often heartfelt expressions of gratitude for His unwavering goodness and mercy. It is this passion that also finds me serving as the choir director in my church, fulfilling the very purpose I was created for. Beyond the church, my everyday life as a graphic designer allows me to express creativity, and with God's continued guidance, my business thrives.

For three transformative years, I had the privilege of serving as President for the Great Lakes Baptist Association Youth Ministry—a truly anointed assignment. God led our efforts, and together, we opened new doors, creating vibrant opportunities for our youth.

I extend this invitation to all, especially the young at heart: pay close attention to the unique purpose imprinted upon your life. Strive to be everything you were designed to be. Listen attentively to the wisdom generously shared with you. Above all, prioritize God in every aspect of your existence. He is the Alpha and the Omega, the Creator of all things, and He will undeniably lead you down the righteous path. "Won't God do it?" Indeed, He will.

Theme: Fighter

1 Timothy 6:12 KJV

Fight the good fight of faith, lay hold on eternal life, whereunto thou art also called, and hast professed a good profession before many witnesses.

_____

_____

_____

_____

_____

_____

_____

_____

_____

_____

_____

Zipporah Anyanna Ross is the youngest daughter of Pastor Franklin and First Lady Goldie Ross.

Zipporah's Christian journey started at Holy Trinity Missionary Baptist Church, where she served on the usher board, praised and worshipped God through the dance/flag ministry, and the youth and young adult choir.

She's a graduate of Monroe Community College, where she obtained an Associate degree in Liberal Arts and Sciences: General Studies.

In 2013, she was baptized and later moved her membership to Peace Missionary Baptist Church (PMBC), where her father was called to be their pastor.

She serves as a youth advisor, member of the culinary and hospitality ministry, and has previously served as the co-director of the PMBC Youth choir. She also assists with the assembling of church and community food baskets.

In July 2024, she was the recipient of the Young Adult Servant Leader Award from the Great Lakes Baptist Association Young People's Auxiliary.

Her community activities included her being a volunteer for AKOMA, an all-female African American gospel choir,
Pearlessence 30 years of Praise Scholarship Concert.

Fighting Fear with Faith by Zipporah Anyanna Ross

"Fear thou not; for I am with thee: be not dismayed; for I am thy God: I will strengthen thee: yea, I will help thee; yea, I will uphold thee with the right hand of my righteousness."

Isaiah 41:10 KJV

Sometime in October 2014, while driving to a friend's house, my grandfather's heart suddenly stopped beating, and this led to him being in a coma. At first, it took me a while to process what exactly was going on. It wasn't until I saw my family in the ICU waiting room that the feeling of fear snuck up on me. Fearful and anxious thoughts started filling my head like "How long would he be like this?" or "What if he doesn't make it?" and "How would my family recover from this?" And after a couple of nurses wanted us to be aware that patients usually don't survive something like this, and we should give it a month, then pull the plug, just making those thoughts louder. In a way, I was letting the fear control me.

Instead of dealing with what I was feeling and thinking, I just suppressed it and put on this mask that I was okay. Anytime my parents and I went to visit him, I would avoid going into his room by staying in the waiting room with other family members. That feeling of fear weighed me down for some time during his hospitalization. One day, while I was in the library, working on something for class, those thoughts started to find their way back into my mind. I guess emotionally and mentally, I had had enough because I began to cry and even question why this was happening to my family.

Taking a minute to check myself and remind myself of what God had done for my family in previous situations, that if He did it then, then He'll do it again. Later that night, instead of staying in the waiting room, my cousin took my hand and we went to my grandfather's room. My cousin was the one who held his hand and started talking to him. Shortly after that, my grandfather squeezed her hand. There was a nurse in the room who had seen what had happened and tried to tell us that it was just a "muscle spasm", but I just rolled my eyes because I knew otherwise. I knew that was God, and the weight from the fear I was experiencing earlier had been lifted. From then on, my grandfather would improve more and more, returning to his old self.

In April 2024, we laid him to rest. That's ten additional years that those doctors and even some of the nurses did not expect. That's ten more years of him driving, fishing, and sharing his "special" wisdom. Knowing that his transition was on God's time and not on man's has brought me some comfort. Looking back, I ponder how this experience has shaped my faith into the person I am today. I also ponder how far God has brought not just me, but my family's faith as well.

These are things that I had to (and still do) keep in mind whenever fear shows up that might help you;

1.) Stay prayed up. Anytime that fearful thinking starts to creep up on you, pray, or when you feel like nothing seems to be working, pray, for there is power in prayer.

2.) Remember whose child you are. Philippians 4:13 (KJV) reads, *I can do all things through Christ, which strengtheneth me,* meaning that when it feels like you're getting kicked around by fear, know that God gave you the strength to kick it right back.

3.) Read the Word. In the bible, you will come across many scriptures that address conquering fear, like Deuteronomy 31:6, Joshua 1:9, or the 23rd Psalm, just to name a few.

4.) Keep the faith. Don't lose faith in yourself, but most importantly, don't lose faith in God.

5.) Get help. Whenever fear attempts to take control and those fearful thoughts are hanging above your head, reach out and

67

get help. Whether that maybe talking to your pastor or even reaching out to a therapist (yes, I said it!), don't hesitate.

You know that saying "there's a first time for everything," well, this would be it. The experience I had during my grandfather's hospitalization was the first time I had to acknowledge the struggle I have with fear and anxiety. I'm starting to see that by sharing my struggle with others, it allows them to see that they are not alone. Also, it shows them not to give in to it, that they should keep going, and they should put their trust in the Lord. My prayer is that even people who aren't struggling with fear and anxiety will see that they can overcome any obstacle life throws at them, with the help of God. Ongoing, that's the word I'd use to describe my message about my life. I chose this word because life is an ongoing journey, even when every day is a constant battle. However, I know that with God on my side, I can and will conquer whatever that day may hold.

If you want to reach out to me, email me: zaross1@outlook.com.

Theme: Faithfulness

Hebrews 10:23 KJV

Let us hold fast the profession of our faith without wavering; (for he is faithful that promised;)

_____

_____

_____

_____

_____

_____

_____

My name is **Stefanie Kerr**. I was born on **January 23, 1984** - yes, that means I'm the 1, 2, and 3. Born in **Hartford, Kentucky**, but proudly **raised in Buffalo, New York**, I am the mother of three amazing children - **Davon, Kyra, and Kylee** - and the G to one very special grandbaby, **Karter**.

After many years of working with children in different capacities, I am now the **Program Director of the Drop-In Center for Children in the 2 Court Building**. Every day, I provide care, services, and resources for families with children from six weeks to twelve years old. I never take it lightly, because I've walked in many of the same shoes as those I serve.

The Inception — Becoming the Woman God Designed by Stefanie Kerr

"The stone the builders rejected has become the cornerstone." —
Psalm 118:22

I give all thanks to God, because my life has not been a walk in the park. There were many days I wanted to hand Him both the shoes and the shoulders that carried so much weight. The shoes were big, and at times, they felt far too big for me.

I remember those days so clearly - being a full-time high school student, raising my three-year-old, managing my own apartment, and still thinking, *"Maybe I need another job."* My mornings started early: getting my son ready for daycare, catching the yellow school bus, and heading to the Buffalo Academy for Visual and Performing Arts. After school, I'd rush to work at Burger King, trying to make ends meet.

Sundays were for church, no matter how tired I was, I sang in the choir, attended Sunday school, and brought my son right along with me. If the church doors were open, we were there. That's where I found peace, even when I was battling storms no one could see. But if I'm honest, there came a time when I was angry - angry at life, at my situation, at God. I was tired of the whispers and the stares, tired of feeling like my mistakes were louder than my prayers. This wasn't the life I planned. I wanted so much more - and the more I wanted, the harder it felt to reach.

There were days I truly didn't think I would make it. I failed almost every year and spent my summers in school trying to catch up. Still, somehow, God always made a way. Looking back, I realize He had rams in the bushes waiting for me, people who showed up right when I needed them most. There were teachers, church members, and quiet encouragers who helped carry me and my child when I was too weary to carry myself.

Yet for every person who prayed for me, there were others who tried to tear me down, to remind me of where I came from instead of where I was going. But even their doubt became fuel. Every time someone said I couldn't, I silently promised myself that I would.

Life began shaping me long before I understood what true strength meant. Becoming a teen mother changed everything. In one moment, my world shifted from innocence to responsibility. While others my age were planning futures, I was learning to hold one in my arms.

Marriage came quickly, along with the hope of stability and love. But the weight of youth, responsibility, and expectation became heavy. I was still discovering who I was while trying to be everything to everyone else — a wife, a mother, a provider, and a woman of faith.

Through every season, **church and God were the foundation of my life**. I grew up surrounded by strong, praying women — giant women of faith in my family and my church who believed that no matter what storm came, God would carry us through. Their prayers often covered me when I couldn't find the words to pray for myself. Yet even with that faith, there were nights I looked up and asked, *"Why me?"*

I often wondered why God placed such heavy crosses on my shoulders, and why my struggles seemed so visible. It felt like my pain was on display for others to witness, and I questioned His purpose for my suffering. But one Sunday, my pastor preached a message that changed my heart forever. He said, *"Why not you?"*

That moment hit me deeply. For the first time, I began to understand that this struggle — my journey of early motherhood, marriage, divorce, and perseverance — was not meant to destroy me. It was designed to shape me, to prepare me to help others, and to be living proof that God still performs miracles. That message became a turning point in my faith.

Music became my refuge. Singing in church was my escape, my form of prayer. My favorite song was *"I've Seen Him Work,"* beautifully sung by the late Sarah Cook and Daisy Nolley. I would pour out every bit of my hurt, my pain, my fears, and my tears through those soprano notes. That song became my testimony before I even knew it. Each time I sang it, I felt God speaking to me, reminding me that He was still in control, still working things out for my good.

My old pastor, **James Blackburn**, used to say, *"God has a way with promises; He keeps them."* Over the years, I've seen that to be true. There were times when I had to apply every lesson I was ever taught, going into my prayer closet, cleaning my house, playing my gospel music loud, and praying and crying all at once. Some days, I didn't know where the strength or the help was going to come from. Some days I **dressed my stress well**, smiling through the struggle. Other days, I ran from it, thinking I could hide. Depression dragged me down, but even then, God was there.

Those were the moments that reminded me: even when I tried to hold it all together, God saw the truth beneath the surface. He met me in those hidden places, right between my tears and my prayers.

Psalm 118 became my anchor. When I felt rejected by circumstances and overwhelmed by responsibility, I held tight to the promise that what others overlook, God can build upon. Even when my plans crumbled, He was laying the foundation for something new.

Those years taught me resilience, faith, and courage. They became the birthplace of my strength — **the inception of who I was becoming.**

Looking back, I see now that every tear I shed, every night I felt alone, was shaping me for what was next. Strength didn't come easy it came through the hard, messy, beautiful process of holding on when I had nothing left. I started as a young girl just trying to survive, but God was quietly turning me into a woman who could thrive. He was teaching me to rise, to walk in purpose, and to be a light for others even when I couldn't see it myself, and as this chapter closes, I step forward with hope, ready for the next season, trusting that He's already at work in ways I can't yet imagine.

He Turned It

For ten years, it was just me and my son exploring the world together, trying to find our place in it. Life started to look a little brighter. I promised myself I wouldn't have another child until I was married. But there I was - pregnant again, dating, and wondering, *"How did I get here? What am I going to do?"*

I wanted to be the one to break the generational curse to finally succeed, to do it differently. But somehow, it felt like I was stuck in the middle of the same spinning wheel. Years later, we decided to get married. I had no desire to be just another "baby mama." Despite the red flags, I believed my prayers and faithfulness would bless our union. I thought, *"Surely, if I keep doing what's right, God will make this work."*

After many prayers, He did bring us back to church as a family. We joined **Friendship Baptist Church** under the leadership of **Pastor Edward Jackson**. We were active and involved. We prayed together, attended service every Sunday, and served wherever we could. I believed this was the answered prayer that God was finally *working it out.*

I began to pray about opening my own daycare. I had worked in so many over the years and knew that world like the back of my hand. The Bible says, *"He is a rewarder of those who diligently seek Him,"* and I held onto that promise. I searched, prayed, and drew closer to God. I began to feel His presence like never before. I thought, *"All the pain I've endured, He's finally turning it into purpose."* And just like that, with one phone call, everything fell into place.

We wanted that "God-given perfect family," the one without worries, without storms. But then, after three miscarriages, came my miracle. My baby arrived three months early, weighing just one pound. Out of nowhere, a new journey began. I remember crying, *"My God, my God — why this cup? Haven't I endured enough hurt, pain, and struggle?"*

The day of her birth was terrifying. I went to the ER because something didn't feel right. After receiving IV fluids, I was being discharged, but in a few short minutes, I went into labor. As my emergency C-section began, the doctors rushed, asking questions about my health and making me sign paperwork for blood transfusions and resuscitation for both myself and my baby.

As they prepared me for anesthesia, the doctor said, *"Count backward."* Frantically, I couldn't remember what number came before ten. I whispered, *"Jesus."* The doctor responded, *"Well, say Jesus."* I prayed as I drifted to sleep because He was the only One I could call.

When I woke, the doctor came to me and said, *"Your Jesus was in the room."* The textbooks said my baby shouldn't survive, but Jesus was there, literally in the corner of the operating room. I have never experienced anything like it. Kylee is now 11 years old, healthy, breathing on her own, and thriving — a true miracle and testament to God's presence.

I couldn't understand it at the time. My marriage was crumbling, my daycare had to close, and my children needed me in different ways. One child was fighting for her life in the hospital, and I was stretched beyond what I thought I could bear. I needed help more than ever, but I didn't know how to ask. I was ashamed and exhausted — torn between being a home mom and a hospital mom.

Many days I sat alone at the hospital, praying out loud, crying until I had no more words. I read my Bible for myself, not just for comfort but for understanding. I quoted scriptures and phrases I had heard all my life, but they felt empty - until one Sunday, something changed.

Pastor Jackson was preaching, and I found myself at the altar, crying out. Then he looked my way and said, *"Your gift is making room for you."* He nodded at me, and it was like I was the only person in the sanctuary. Something inside me shifted. It didn't happen overnight, but the unbearable became bearable. I started walking in my purpose, no longer ashamed of my story.

And then - God turned it.

My finances changed. A job came through. The right people began to appear, and the wrong ones fell away. God placed me in spaces and positions I didn't have the credentials for - but I had the knowledge, the care, the compassion, and the empathy that couldn't be taught.

He reminded me of His promise: *"Delight yourself in the Lord, and He will give you the desires of your heart."* And truly, all I ever wanted was to be happy.

It rained, but I didn't drown. Every storm came to strengthen me, not to destroy me. I didn't look like what I'd been through, not like a teen mom, not like a divorced woman carrying wounds. I looked like Grace.

Because I am Stefanie, a fighter, a prayer warrior, a believer, and an encourager, every trial, every storm, every prayer has shaped me into who I am today. The journey continues, but God's hand is evident in every step, and my story is His testimony.

Theme: Inception

2 Corinthians 5:17 KJV

Therefore, if any man be in Christ, he is a new creature: old things are passed away; behold, all things are become new.

_____

_____

_____

_____

_____

_____

_____

_____

_____

_____

_____

_____

_____

_____

_____

_____

_____

_____

_____

My name is Nicole Blackburn. I am the daughter of Anthony and Michele. I have two brothers named Anthony Jr. and Reginald. I also have a nephew, Jayden. I grew up and am still a proud member of the Greater Hope Baptist Church. It was there that I became a junior usher and sang in the choir from a young age. It is because of the great teachings of my Pastor and Sunday School Teachers, I developed a heart for serving others through teaching.

My first teaching position was in the church. My journey as a Sunday school teacher deepened my faith and encouraged me to become an educator. I am very proud of the successes I have achieved throughout my life. Throughout college, I was a dedicated tutor to kids in my neighborhood. I helped many students unlock their full potential and become passionate learners.

I graduated from Buffalo State with my Elementary Education degree. I also received my Master's there in Urban Education. My first position was working for a Buffalo, NY charter school. I am honored to now work for Lackawanna Schools. I count it a blessing to serve and work in the very city I was raised.

God has blessed me to be able to pour into the community in which I live. I am dedicated to being a teacher who lifts students up and makes learning meaningful. I believe in making reading accessible and fun.

I placed full bookshelves in barbershops in western New York to help boys discover the joy of reading. I am blessed to have a supportive family. They are one of my greatest blessings. I cherish their laughs, support, and prayers. They are truly a gift and a testimony. Not only my family, but I am truly blessed to have a supportive group of friends.

I thank them for encouraging me or simply laughing with me along this journey. I am so grateful for the community of love that surrounds me. God has been so good to me.

Walking With The Promise Keeper: Living in God's Faithfulness by Nicole Blackburn

"God has a way with promises. He keeps them." -Pastor James C.

Blackburn Jr.

It was Sunday, May 21st, 2023. 10 days after I got my new bright red truck. 60 days before the end of the school year. The day after my cousin's graduation party. 1 day before my life was changed "forever". After church, my mom and my cousins were cleaning up after we hosted a graduation party. I decided to have some leftovers from the party. Fried chicken. I warmed it up for one minute and thirty seconds. My family was in the garage, so I decided to take my food out there. I started to eat and felt this feeling I'd never felt before. A feeling I still can't explain. The only thing I can remember was my family staring at me with a concerned look. "Cole, are you okay?" I didn't know how to respond. What just happened? What was that feeling? I let them know I was fine. I threw out my chicken and went to the living room. After that moment, I slept for more than an hour.

Once I woke up, I asked my mom what all that was about. She said I stood there with a blank look and kept repeating "I'm sorry". Eventually, I told them all I was tired. To myself, I said, "Well, at least I was speaking". My mom and I both agreed that maybe I just needed my after church nap and was a bit stressed about going back to work on Monday. I finished up my weekly lesson plans and went to bed early.

This was my first year at a new school. The school I wanted to work at desperately. I wanted to be perfect at my job. I had a very tough class, and it felt like everyone was watching me to see how I would handle them. The class had a majority of boys, which was hard to handle, but there was one who made my day even more challenging. He never followed directions. He tried to make everyone laugh at the wrong times. The constant interruptions not only made it hard to teach but also made it hard for me to think. Had a supportive mentor and a couple of friends who helped me through the year, but it still felt more than tough. I would come home daily, discussing my time at work with my parents. I was beyond stressed.

It is now Monday, May 22nd, 2023. I cannot stop thinking about what happened yesterday. I had taken my class to an assembly in the school gym. They were so excited to be there. As I sat there, in my own thoughts, I began to silently cry. Did I have a stroke yesterday? Do I have cancer? What was that? I need to leave! I walked to my assistant principal. I told him everything and ended with, "I can't make it through the rest of the day". He understood completely. He found a substitute, and I left. Little did I know, I wouldn't be back for another 2 weeks. I got in my truck and called my mom. I expressed all my worries to her, and she called my brother Reggie. God help me!

I drove to Reggie's house, and he drove me to Erie County Medical Center. On the way there, I was hysterically crying. He is doing his best to calm me down and help control my breathing. Once we arrived at the ER, I was seen very quickly. The ER workers were ready to receive me. The nurses and doctors were very thorough. They determined I did not have a stroke. Thank You Jesus! I did not have any tumors. Hallelujah! I began to calm down. Maybe this was just a silly worry. "Nicole, you're having seizures". What?

I have never had any health issues before. Nothing "bad" had ever happened in my life. After that, I stayed in the hospital for four days. My wonderful cousin, one of the head nurses there, was able to get me my own room. My hospital stay was lovely, but the thoughts that went through my head were not. Why me, Lord? I've been faithful to You, but You do me like this? My family came to see me during my stay and sent many encouraging text messages, but none of that eased the hurt I was experiencing. God, are You there?

The bad news just kept rolling in. Now, my brand-new truck needs to be put away. You have to be 6 months seizure-free before you can drive again. How can this happen when I seize when I eat? The school year is not over either. After all of this, I still have to go back to my classroom. My dad took me and picked me up from work every day. I cried every morning and every night. Why me, Lord?

As the year passes, I learn more and more about my condition. I found out that if I have a seizure, it happens when I eat. They happen in the left temporal lobe of my brain. I learned that my medication will cause me to lose my balance. I found out what medications don't work, which ones cause an allergic reaction, and which ones give me a horrible headache. I try other things to control my seizures, CBD gummies, gluten gluten-free diet, or diabetes patches. None of which worked. Where are You, Jesus?

This moment in life caused me to not only lose faith in myself, but also in God. How could I trust someone I can't see with my own eyes or hear with my ears? I felt I couldn't talk to Him, because He obviously was not listening. I cried to my friends, family, and coworkers, everybody except Him. I was stress eating and went into a depression. I gained over 50 pounds. My support system was wonderful listeners, but what I was going through internally was something I couldn't share. I hated myself and the way I looked. The plan I had for my healing and happiness was not working. God, I can't take this!

There were days I woke up crying and went to bed crying. There were days without seizures, and there were days with seizures. Then sometimes with more than one. A change in my personality was evident. Everyone asked, "Cole, how is everything going"? Quickly, I'd say "I'm good". If I shared my true feelings, I wouldn't be able to stop crying. There isn't enough time in the day to share how I am REALLY feeling. Then, my primary care doctor asked me how I was doing. I responded to him, "I'm good". My wonderful doctor saw right through me. He knew that with everything I am experiencing, there is no way "I'm good". Of course, I broke down crying. He then told me, not suggested, but told me, it is time to see a therapist.

Therapy? I thought only crazy people go to therapy. That is far from the truth. Therapy is for anyone who wants to feel better, grow, and heal. People go to therapy for all kinds of reasons. Stress, anxiety, low motivation, and many others. I then had to accept that I needed help. I am living with something that has caused me to slip into negative thoughts.

I needed to talk to someone whom I wouldn't be embarrassed to cry in front of. Someone who can give me strategies to relax my mind when life gets stressful. My therapist has given me the tools to see life's challenges differently. She taught me that there are things in life you can't control, even though it's extremely difficult. We all go through stress or anxiety. This may lead to automatic thoughts of uncertainty.

I had to learn to tolerate uncertain situations. As I pondered that beneficial and truthful idea, I learned something else. I had been stressed because I felt God did not love me. I was searching for God daily. Then it hit me, He was always there, and this is all a part of His will; a will that I had to trust.

Trust His will, Trust His timing, and Trust His promises.

Therapy helped me realize that I wanted control over my situation. None of us knows what tomorrow is going to bring. We have plans for our lives, but we truly do not know what is to come. I had no clue that I would be taking seizure medication day and night. Yes, I can cry, but I should not worry because I serve a faithful God who keeps His promises. Mathew 6:34 KJV states, "Take therefore no thought for the morrow, for the morrow shall take thought for the things of itself. Sufficient unto the day is the evil thereof". I thought I knew how to trust the Lord, until a storm came into my life. Trusting God to completely take care of me has been the hardest thing I have had to accept.

How can I trust someone I cannot see? My fears came from my trying to carry this load alone. My pastor reminded me that I am never alone. The Lord knows how to take care of you. Therapy guided me to surrender my worries to God. I was reminded by my pastor that God makes promises in His word. Unlike humans, God always keeps His promises. It was time to trust the Lord. It was time to let go and let God lead. It was time to grow in God.

There are many people in this world who are experiencing this alone. The Lord has blessed me with family and friends to support me. Had I been physically alone throughout this, I can't say I would be here today. Life can feel uneasy at times, like the struggle will never end. For those who are physically alone in a storm, I encourage you to find someone to talk to. Also, never believe that God is not there. Not only did I have physical support around me, but I realized that God was there the entire time. I thought I started this journey without Christ. I thought He wanted me to fight this battle alone. I questioned His presence daily. I thought I couldn't open up to Him. I felt defeated. On the contrary, He gave me all the attention I needed. We can go to Him for anything.

God makes a promise in Hebrews 13:5. It states, "I will never leave you nor forsake you". No matter what you are experiencing, God promised He will never abandon you. Never means "not at all". There is never a reason to doubt that He is there. It will feel like you're going through all alone, but God is right by your side. In moments of overwhelming fear, we can hold on to the promise that God is always there. Thank you, Lord, for being with me wherever I go (Joshua 1:9).

I told the Lord many times that I am unable to go on. My everyday struggles take a toll on me mentally and physically. I wondered how long this would be, because I am tired. I failed to see that the Lord gave me the strength to make it through every day. Isaiah says in Isaiah 40:29 KJV that the Lord gives power to the faint. I was more than faint. But the Lord supplied every need I had (Philippians 4:19).

No matter how uncertain life feels, trust and believe God is going to give you everything you need. The Lord is faithful to give us everything we could ever ask for. As I think about my story, the Lord has given more than I needed in His own time. I needed Him to answer me at that moment. I figured, since I grew up a Christian, I go to church every Sunday, and I love Him. He should answer my prayers quickly. Right? No, that's not how the Lord works. I wanted Him right now, but He was telling me to wait.

While waiting on the Lord, I have said some unkind and unloving things to Him. I fell short and made mistakes. Yet, He showed me grace and mercy (Romans 5:20). This is not because I deserve it, but because of His promise of love. Now, I am strong in the Lord! My faithful Lord has taught me that patience means to wait on Him. To allow Him to fix it. Trust his faithful timing. I'm built to last, all because of the faithfulness of my Savior. God, thank you for being a God of grace and mercy.

Days came when I couldn't stop worrying about what would happen to me next. Worry crept into my mind daily. I constantly asked my doctors and family, "What if...". I constantly asked my Savior, "Why?". Worry snatched joy and peace out of my life. Stress took over my life. I was so stressed that it made me sick. I held on to all of my worries when I should've released them all to God. Jeremiah 29:11 KJV "For I know the thoughts that I think toward you, saith the Lord, thoughts of peace and not of evil to give you an expected end".

The Lord made this promise. No good comes to you by worrying. I realized that I only gain a headache by worrying. In stressful seasons, God has a plan for our good. Instead of worrying, I should seek the Promise Keeper. We need to give all of our worries to God in prayer.

When things happen, it's all a part of God's will. It's our job to let go and let Him work. That is a difficult thing to do, but my pastor once said, "Stop fighting God and let Him work it out". God's will is perfect. God, I may not always understand everything You're doing, but I trust You.

God's will is a difficult thing to trust. Another word for God's will is God's plan. I wanted to work on my plan and find easy ways to fix my problem. I had to learn how to release all control and believe in His plan. I quickly learned that if you don't follow God's plan, you don't receive the blessings that He plans to give you. When you allow the Lord to work in your life and do what He commands, He will pour out blessings that you will have no room to receive (Malachi 3:10). Jesus taught us in The Lord's Prayer to say, "Your will be done". We are all choosing to release our control and be under His. Even when the path looks rocky, we should trust Him. The Lord knows how to take care of you. You must let go of the control you think you have over your life. God is in full control of our lives. He knew everything about us before we were born. We may not know what or why He is doing the things He does. It is not our job to figure that out. His will or plan for our life is fixed in love. Even when life feels confusing, God promised to give us peace when we trust Him (Isaiah 26:3). Do not fear or be discouraged. Peace is kept by only keeping your heart and mind on God and His will. I thought I was living alright until I realized Jesus wants me. Now I understand the lesson the Lord was teaching me in this season. He taught me to trust Him to stay near me in difficult and glad experiences. Lord, thank You for showing me You are in full control. Lord, I'm relying on You.

For so long, I thought God was mad at me because I did something wrong in life, and He was punishing me. I wondered if His promises really applied to me. What I learned is that I have taken God's faithfulness for granted throughout my life. I mistook my trials for His silence. I thought I walked through this test alone, but God was always there. He is completely faithful. He never left my side. His word remains the same, and He keeps His promises.

For many days, I questioned God's love for me. When I should've told Him thank you for his never-failing love. Worrying is an easy thing to do. Doubting that God is at your side is also an easy thing to do. Pastor and author Mark Littleton once said, "Turn your doubts to questions; turn your questions to prayers; turn your prayers to God". Don't let your doubts keep you from talking to the faithful Promise Keeper.

If your worries have you questioning God's faithfulness, read Lamentations 3:22-23. We must pray with our eyes on our God and not on our worries. Trust that your faithful God is in full control. When I worry, I now pray for forgiveness. God is faithful to forgive every time (1 John 1:19). It doesn't matter how long you've done wrong. As you confess your sins, He forgives them. God never promised that life would be easy, but He promised to never leave me. He promised there would be joy. He promised that I would have peace if I trusted Him. He promised to give me the strength to endure.

The Lord is faithful and has a plan for all of our lives. Yes, He is faithful to us, but we need to be faithful to Him as well. The best place to be is in the will of God. My pastor said one Sunday, "Work the plan and it will turn your life around". Follow the Lord's plan for your life. I encourage you to find a promise from God and keep it in your heart. There are hundreds of promises in scripture. Every promise of God is yes for those who believe and trust in Him. Even when you can't see Him, He is there.

Our faithful God promised that He stays close to us. When life starts to get you down, I encourage you to remember the goodness of the Lord. When life gets hard, think about what God has done for you. What wonderful works has He done in your life? Remind yourself that He is a faithful God who continues to bless you daily. Then, lift your hands and give Him praise.

Nobody knows what the future will bring, but we do know who holds the future. His promises are not based on your perfection, but we should work to be more like Christ every day. His faithfulness and love are promised to us. Doubt doesn't ban us from His promises. It is an invitation to grow nearer to our faithful Lord and Savior. Let go of your worries and trust the Promise Keeper. He will give you the victory.

Theme: Shift

Romans 12:2 KJV

And be not conformed to this world: but be ye transformed by the renewing of your mind, that ye may prove what is that good, and acceptable, and perfect, will of God.

Biblical Resources:
King James Version(KJV)

The Lord's Prayer
Matthew 6:9-14 KJV

After this manner, therefore pray ye: Our Father which art in heaven, Hallowed be thy name. Thy kingdom come. Thy will be done in earth, as it is in heaven. Give us this day our daily bread. And forgive us our debts, as we forgive our debtors. And lead us not into temptation, but deliver us from evil: For thine is the kingdom, and the power, and the glory, for ever. Amen.

Psalms 23 KJV The

LORD is my shepherd; I shall not want. He

maketh me to lie down in green pastures: he

leadeth me beside the still waters.

He restoreth my soul:

he leadeth me in the paths of righteousness for his name's sake.

Yea, though I walk through the valley of the shadow of death, I

will fear no evil: for thou art with me; thy rod and thy staff

comfort me.

Thou preparest a table before me in the presence of mine enemies:

thou anointest my head with oil; my cup runneth over.

Surely goodness and mercy shall follow me all the days of my life: and

I will dwell in the house of the LORD for ever.

The Beatitudes

Matthew 5:3-12 KJV

Blessed are the poor in spirit: for theirs is the kingdom of heaven.

Blessed are they that mourn: for they shall be comforted.

Blessed are the meek: for they shall inherit the earth.

Blessed are they which do hunger and thirst after righteousness: for they shall be filled.

Blessed are the merciful: for they shall obtain mercy.

Blessed are the pure in heart: for they shall see God.

Blessed are the peacemakers: for they shall be called the children of God.

Blessed are they which are persecuted for righteousness' sake: for theirs is the kingdom of heaven.

Blessed are ye, when men shall revile you, and persecute you, and shall say all manner of evil against you falsely, for my sake.

Rejoice, and be exceeding glad: for great is your reward in heaven: for so persecuted they the prophets which were before you.

The Armor Of God

Ephesians 6:1-18 KJV

Finally, my brethren, be strong in the Lord, and in the power of his might. Put on the whole armour of God, that ye may be able to stand against the wiles of the devil. For we wrestle not against flesh and blood, but against principalities, against powers, against the rulers of the darkness of this world, against spiritual wickedness in high places. Wherefore take unto you the whole armour of God, that ye may be able to withstand in the evil day, and having done all, to stand.

Stand therefore, having your loins girt about with truth, and having on the breastplate of righteousness; And your feet shod with the preparation of the gospel of peace; Above all, taking the shield of faith, wherewith ye shall be able to quench all the fiery darts of the wicked.

And take the helmet of salvation, and the sword of the Spirit, which is the word of God: Praying always with all prayer and supplication in the Spirit, and watching thereunto with all perseverance and supplication for all saints;

The Golden Rule

Matthew 7:12 KJV

Therefore, all things whatsoever ye would that men should do to you, do ye even so to them: for this is the law and the prophets.

The Ten Commandments

Exodus 20:1-17

And God spake all these words, saying, I am the LORD thy God, which have brought thee out of the land of Egypt, out of the house of bondage. Thou shalt have no other gods before me. Thou shalt not make unto thee any graven image, or any likeness of any thing that is in heaven above, or that is in the earth beneath, or that is in the water under the earth: Thou shalt not bow down thyself to them, nor serve them: for I the LORD thy God am a jealous God, visiting the iniquity of the fathers upon the children unto the third and fourth generation of them that hate me; And shewing mercy unto thousands of them that love me, and keep my commandments. Thou shalt not take the name of the LORD thy God in vain; for the LORD will not hold him guiltless that taketh his name in vain. Remember the sabbath day, to keep it holy. Six days shalt thou labour, and do all thy work: But the seventh day is the sabbath of the LORD thy God: in it thou shalt not do any work, thou, nor thy son, nor thy daughter, thy manservant, nor thy maidservant, nor thy cattle, nor thy stranger that is within thy gates: For in six days the LORD made heaven and earth, the sea, and all that in them is, and rested the seventh day: wherefore the LORD blessed the sabbath day, and hallowed it.

Honour thy father and thy mother: that thy days may be long upon the land which the LORD thy God giveth thee. Thou shalt not kill. Thou shalt not commit adultery. Thou shalt not steal. Thou shalt not bear false witness against thy neighbour. Thou shalt not covet thy neighbour's house, nor his manservant, nor his maidservant, nor his ox, nor his ass, nor any thing that is thy neighbour's.

Words of Inspiration by Writing Coach Brenda W. Billups

I express my profound appreciation for the opportunity to have served as an assistant on this exceptional book project. My involvement has been an extraordinarily enriching experience, and I am deeply grateful for the insights gained throughout its development.

I have been consistently impressed by the remarkable brilliance and unwavering dedication that have been meticulously invested in every aspect of this endeavor. Witnessing the intricate creative process unfold and being able to contribute, even in a supportive capacity, has been a source of immense inspiration and professional growth.

I eagerly anticipate the upcoming release of this work, confident that its meticulously crafted content will captivate and resonate profoundly with its global audience. This project, in my estimation, stands as a testament to exceptional scholarship and creative execution, poised to become a significant contribution in its field. This book will be an inspiration to all.

Words of Inspiration by Writing Coach Shelia Pinckney

"What shall I render unto the Lord for all his benefits toward me?" This has been my mantra for the past year. Walking with Jesus (often being carried) through the most difficult season of my life, I am learning what it truly means to put my trust in God; to live out the faith I professed (since I was a child) to have when I'm not facing the storms of life.

When I first heard of this project, I immediately felt a call to lend my support. Having worked with children and young people for over thirty years in both my professional and personal life, I know what a great cloud of witnesses they are to what it means to belong to God. The young adults who are courageously sharing their stories on this project have experienced both trials and triumphs in their lives. And while their journeys are varied, they all have in common a desire to help someone else along this faith journey. My prayer is that you will be inspired, encouraged, motivated, and rejuvenated as I have been by their stories.

We all will have doubts, questions, and even fear sometimes in this life. Thank God, we have His Word. We don't have to search the world for wisdom; it's already given to us. I reflect on Ecclesiastes 12:13, which says (I'm paraphrasing), my job is to fear God and keep His commandments. And what is the great commandment? He tells us in Matthew 22:34-40 to love God with all our heart, soul, and mind and love thy neighbor as thyself.

So I don't have to wonder what I shall render to God, and neither do you. Singer/Songwriter Vanessa Bell Armstrong said it best, God has everything and everything belongs to God, so all we have to give is our heart, mind, and soul. And that is how we get the victory already won by Jesus Christ.

Congratulations to these incredible Co-Authors. Your Name is Victory!

To God Be The Glory

Words of Inspiration

Words of Inspiration by Writing Coach Dr. Johnique Billups Atkins

I am deeply inspired by the strength and courage of young adults who have faced life's challenges with resilience and grace. Their stories are often woven with hardship, perseverance, and quiet determination—proof that endurance can be both powerful and gentle. They have navigated change, loss, and reinvention, yet continue to stand tall, offering wisdom and compassion to those who follow. Their courage is not always loud; sometimes it shows in their steady hands, their laughter after sorrow, or their refusal to give up on themselves or others. Watching them reminds me that true strength is built over time, through lived experience and unwavering hope.

Writing has a remarkable power to heal because it allows us to give shape to emotions that might otherwise remain tangled and unspoken. Putting thoughts into words can bring clarity to confusion, helping us process pain, loss, or fear in a safe and private space. Through storytelling, journaling, or even a few honest sentences, writing becomes a release—a way to transform inner chaos into understanding and meaning. It helps us witness our own growth, see patterns in our experiences, and recognize our resilience. In this way, writing is not just expression—it's an act of self-compassion and restoration, a bridge between what hurts and what can be healed.

I am profoundly proud of young adults who choose to write their stories, claiming their voices in a world that has too often tried to silence them. Each word they put on the page is an act of courage – a declaration that their experiences, memories, and perspectives matter. Through writing, they not only honor their own journeys but also create space for others to see themselves reflected, understood, and inspired. Whether their stories speak of struggle, triumph, love, or survival, they contribute to a greater chorus of truth and resilience. These young adults remind us that storytelling is both a power and a legacy, and that by sharing their voices, they help shape a more honest and compassionate world.

I hope this book serves as a source of inspiration for every reader who turns its pages. My greatest wish is that the stories, reflections, and insights within it spark something meaningful – encouraging you to see your own strength, courage, and potential more clearly. May it remind you that growth often comes from challenge, that healing is possible, and that your story, too, has power and purpose. If these words offer even a moment of comfort, motivation, or selfbelief, then this book has done what it was meant to do: to inspire hearts, uplift spirits, and remind us all of the beauty found in resilience and hope.

Words of Inspiration by Writing Coach Jamal Donaldson Briggs

To the remarkable young adults embarking on your unique journeys,

I wanted to share a few reflections that I hope will serve as guiding principles as you navigate the exciting and challenging path ahead. The world awaits your contributions, and your potential is truly limitless.

Cultivate a spirit of unwavering optimism and profound respect. These are not just pleasant traits, but powerful tools that shape your perception of the world and, in turn, how the world perceives you. A positive outlook fuels resilience, allowing you to view obstacles not as dead ends but as opportunities for growth. When combined with genuine respect for yourselves and others – their diverse perspectives, experiences, and aspirations – you foster an environment of collaboration and understanding, which is essential for building meaningful connections and driving impactful change. Life will inevitably present its share of doubts and difficulties. When negative thoughts surface, rather than letting them take root, challenge them.

Reframe them into stepping stones towards your most ambitious dreams. Understand that setbacks are not failures, but valuable lessons. Each challenge overcome, each lesson learned, strengthens your resolve and clarifies your vision. Believe in your capacity to transform adversity into a catalyst for extraordinary achievement.

Your integrity is your most valuable asset. Let your commitments be sacred, and your word, your unbreakable bond. The trust you build through keeping promises, both big and small, forms the bedrock of your reputation. It's how you earn respect, foster reliability, and cultivate deep, lasting relationships, both personally and professionally. When others know they can count on you, you open doors to unparalleled opportunities and build a legacy of honor.

Finally, embrace the call to leadership. This doesn't necessarily mean holding a formal title, but rather demonstrating initiative, empathy, and courage in your daily actions. Lead by example, inspire those around you, and stand up for what is right. Take responsibility, seek innovative solutions, and contribute actively to your communities. Your unique voice and perspective are needed to shape a better future for us all.

I have immense faith in your generation's capacity to innovate, inspire, and create a truly remarkable world. Go forth with purpose, integrity, and an unshakeable belief in yourselves.

With deepest encouragement,

Jamal Briggs

Meet Visionary Author Dr. Carla A. Murphy

Dr. Carla A. Murphy, a native of Buffalo, New York, is the Visionary Author of "Silent Chronicles: My Name Is Victory". She is the daughter of James A. Murphy Jr. and Celestine C. Murphy. She has one brother, James A. Murphy III, a dear aunt Maurice Mason, a loving cousin C. Howie Hodges, Esquire, and four beautiful god-daughters, Gabrielle King, Nia Imari Spencer, Camille Akeema Wilbon, and ShaKya Christopher.

Dr. Carla A. Murphy is the CEO of Uniquely Different Enterprises, and she lives a life of service. She works to alleviate the suffering of others and strives to make life better for people all over the world. Carla resources people of all ages by teaching them how to reinvent themselves while turning their dreams into reality.

She is a proud member of the Greater Hope Baptist Church under the leadership of a National Preacher and Christian Educator, Rev. Dr. James C. Blackburn Jr., where she has attended for fifty years.

She has been honored to serve her Christian Community for over thirty years as the past Greater Hope Baptist Church Youth Director, Youth Sunday School Superintendent, Vacation Bible School Director and

Empire Baptist Missionary Convention of New York State Regional Director, Youth Director, Young People's Auxiliary Director of Conference Logistics, and Leader of the Empire Baptist Congress of Christian Education Annual Retreat Junior High Division.

She previously served the Great Lakes Baptist Association as a Youth Supervisor, Assistant Director, Congress of Christian Education Youth Department, and currently serves as the Great Lakes Baptist District Association Young People's Auxiliary Director.

Dr. Carla A. Murphy is a Member of the Genius Is Common Movement. She has volunteered as a Black Business Expo Olympic Global Ambassador on the Black Business Olympics, where she's had many opportunities to share her greatness with the world in over 200 countries as a Speaker and Moderator on several television and social media platforms.

For two years, she hosted The Carla Murphy Show, which aired on her own Roku Channel, "Uniquely Different TV Network." The themes of the show were Family, Community, Christianity, and Business.

Throughout her career as an Entrepreneur, Investigator, and Human Resources Professional, Carla has been a Co-Host on various Business shows on Roku, UAN TV Network, and Fishbowl Radio Network. She's also been featured on shows on IBM TV.

Dr. Carla is a Published Author and a Self-Discovery and Confidence Life Coach. She has mastered many of her coaching skills from her Coach, the President of TMJ Personal Coaching, Emmy/Clio Award-winning Producer Tommy Morgan Jr., who has helped her to get "unstuck" while getting hired.

She has learned how to embrace her uniqueness from her Mentor, Bruce George, Founder of the Genius is Common Movement and Co-Producer of Def Poetry Jam on HBO, which has allowed her to record Genius is Common videos on various social media platforms.

She has participated in several Masterclasses with her Mentor, Dr. Eric Kelly III., Founder and CEO of the Black Business Olympics, and Dr. Clyde Rivers, the Founder of I Change Nations.

Dr. Carla A. Murphy has written "Intentional Investigation: A Practical Guide to Administrative Investigations for Investigators, Educators, and Human Resource Professionals." She is an Amazon #1 Best Seller Author, as a part of her Mentor, Award Winning Speaker, Trainer, and Coach Barbara H. Smith's book, "Empowering You: It's Your Time." Author, Dr. Carla A. Murphy, has been seen on "US Culture and Style Today", "Culture Zone Europe", "UK Education News Network", and the "Global
Education Journal" in addition to several other publications.

She has been highlighted in magazines such as Start Healthy and Hoinser Women Magazine.

Dr. Carla has traveled around the world, including over twenty countries across four continents. She believes that the world is her address. Carla states that "She set out to make a difference, and you made her make history."

She impacts people around the world to reinvent themselves by investing in themselves. She stresses the importance of utilizing transferable skills to help people move to their next level. Her messages about ways to grow, earn, and learn together have impacted people to discover their uniqueness all across the globe.

Throughout her career, Dr. Carla has been a Co-Host on various Business shows on Roku, UAN TV Network, and Fishbowl Radio Network. She's also been featured on shows on IBM TV.

Uniquely Different Enterprises resources Investigators, Human Resource Professionals, Youngpreneurs, and Business Start-Ups. She teaches people how to reinvent themselves while turning their dreams into reality. She helps people to strengthen their corporate culture. The company was started as a result of job loss. Dr. Carla combined the knowledge, skills, and abilities that she acquired from working in customer service, community relations, childcare, compliance, investigations, and human resources to establish Uniquely Different Enterprises.

In 2023, Dr. Carla participated in the "Live Your Best Life" Conference in Nairobi, Kenya, hosted by Dr. Ruben West, where she was invited to Kenya's Parliament to meet with the Speaker of the National Assembly of the Republic of Kenya. Carla received the iChange Nations ™ Builders In Action Legacy Award.

On June 11, 2025, Carla A. Murphy was awarded an Honorary Doctor of Philosophy in Humanities Degree by Dr. Clyde Rivers on behalf of United Graduate College and Seminary International, which is located in Uganda.

Dr. Carla A. Murphy walks by faith and not by sight, knowing that serving God pays off.

uniquelydifferententerprises@gmail.com

Facebook: Carla A. Murphy

LinkedIn: Carla A. Murphy

YouTube: Carla A. Murphy

www.ingramcontent.com/pod-product-compliance
Lightning Source LLC
LaVergne TN
LVHW021121080426
835509LV00011B/1375